EDGAR WALLACE - THE STANDARD HISTORY OF THE WAR

COMPRISING THE OFFICIAL DESPATCHES FROM GENERAL FRENCH AND STAFF WITH DESCRIPTIVE NARRATIVE INCLUDING THE OFFICIAL DESPATCHES FROM GENERAL FRENCH, FEB. 2—JUNE 15, 1915,

VOL. III. ST ÉLOI-GIVENCHY-YPRES-HILL 60-NEUVE CHAPELLE

Richard Horatio Edgar Wallace was born on the 1st April 1875 in Greenwich, London. Leaving school at 12 because of truancy, by the age of fifteen he had experience; selling newspapers, as a worker in a rubber factory, as a shoe shop assistant, as a milk delivery boy and as a ship's cook.

By 1894 he was engaged but broke it off to join the Infantry being posted to South Africa. He also changed his name to Edgar Wallace which he took from Lew Wallace, the author of Ben-Hur.

In Cape Town in 1898 he met Rudyard Kipling and was inspired to begin writing. His first collection of ballads, The Mission that Failed! was enough of a success that in 1899 he paid his way out of the armed forces in order to turn to writing full time.

By 1904 he had completed his first thriller, The Four Just Men. Since nobody would publish it he resorted to setting up his own publishing company which he called Tallis Press.

In 1911 his Congolese stories were published in a collection called Sanders of the River, which became a bestseller. He also started his own racing papers, Bibury's and R. E. Walton's Weekly, eventually buying his own racehorses and losing thousands gambling. A life of exceptionally high income was also mirrored with exceptionally large spending and debts.

Wallace now began to take his career as a fiction writer more seriously, signing with Hodder and Stoughton in 1921. He was marketed as the 'King of Thrillers' and they gave him the trademark image of a trilby, a cigarette holder and a yellow Rolls Royce. He was truly prolific, capable not only of producing a 70,000 word novel in three days but of doing three novels in a row in such a manner. It was in, estimating that by 1928 one in four books being read was written by Wallace, for alongside his famous thrillers he wrote variously in other genres, including science fiction, non-fiction accounts of WWI which amounted to ten volumes and screen plays. Eventually he would reach the remarkable total of 170 novels, 18 stage plays and 957 short stories.

Wallace became chairman of the Press Club which to this day holds an annual Edgar Wallace Award, rewarding 'excellence in writing'.

Diagnosed with diabetes his health deteriorated and he soon entered a coma and died of his condition and double pneumonia on the 7th of February 1932 in North Maple Drive, Beverly Hills. He was buried near his home in England at Chalklands, Bourne End, in Buckinghamshire.

Index Of Contents

CHAPTER I — THE FIGHT FOR YPRES

"As I close this despatch," wrote Sir John French in his memorable despatch of November 20th, "there are signs in evidence that we are possibly in the last stages for the battle of Ypres-Armentières." But for many weary weeks longer the struggle was to continue. Nothing on the scale of the great and disastrous effort of the Prussian Guards which shattered the German hopes to break through the Allied lines was witnessed, but many a severe and desperate encounter took place. The Germans were no longer on the offensive, it had become impossible for them to get round the flank of the Allies, whose lines stretched to the sea. If, therefore, they were to proceed they must pierce the Allies' lines at some point. The despairing effort of the Prussian Guards probably convinced the higher German Command that not much hope lay that way. From that moment the offensive passed to the Allies.

Although the offensive had now passed to the Allies, it was not to be expected that there would be an immediate advance to a decisive attack. The time for that was not yet. The position was almost an unparalleled one in the history of warfare; the extraordinary number of combatants engaged, the length of the opposing lines stretching from the sea coast to the frontier of Switzerland, the immense stretch of trenches of the opposing forces, the unprecedented nature of the weapons; the whole line resembling an endless fortress. It was a new kind of war and demanded a new kind of strategy and novel tactics. The airmen also played a new part, giving gunners precise information of which the accuracy and effectiveness of modern weapons were quick to take full advantage. We shall see in the course of this narrative what deadly work could be done under these novel conditions, and how much was yet to be accomplished before the Allies' offensive could become really effective. It was going on all the time, and of what the Allies' stubborn work meant in endurance and heroism I hope to give some idea.

Meantime the district round Ypres was still the scene of fierce combat.

We know fairly well the extraordinary reason which led the Kaiser and his Generals to concentrate their attentions upon this unhappy town. Ypres represented the last rallying point of citizenship in Belgium. Nearly all the other towns in this great country, great in spirit and in soul if not in acres, were either in the enemy's hands or were battered into confused heaps of brick and mortar. At Ypres by the beginning of December the enemy approached so close that he could bring his smaller howitzers to work and reduce the pride of the ages to smoking ruins. Attack and counter-attack had been the order of the day. Entrenchments hastily dug had been elaborated until they were permanent earthworks, and a succession of charges made by the flower of the German Army was thrown back in confusion. Sometimes the controlling force directing the British operations would order an advance, and slipping their bayonets from their sheaths and fixing them to the muzzles of their rifles, thousands of men would creep out from their earth defence, and moving forward cautiously, availing themselves of every bit of cover, would finally, in one reckless charge, work their way into the enemy's line.

On one wet night, 35 men of a regiment, taking advantage of a pitiless downpour, moved stealthily forward on an advance trench of the enemy, and reached their objective without a shot being fired. It was cold-blooded bayonet work for ten minutes, and the little party retired, having wrecked the trench, leaving behind 20 dead. No one knew what object was served—-it was all part of the general scheme planned and ordered miles and miles away. There, in some quaint little town, occupying what houses were available, was the General Staff. Here were big rooms filled with large-scale maps, where the position of every British unit was marked, and where, with remarkable accuracy, every detail concerning the enemy's strength was also displayed. There was one portion of the Intelligence Department of the General Staff which had nothing else to do but to examine the shoulder badges and the collar ornaments and the various parts of the equipment of dead German soldiers. From this slight evidence these patient men would piece together not only the numbers of the regiments, but the Army Corps and the Army to which they were attached. Every change that the German made in his dispositions had been revealed by this painstaking method, and in consequence the British Commander has always been prepared for every fresh development.

To Headquarters, too, came the thousands of reports from various parts of the field. It was in telephonic communication with London, and in addition there was a large telegraph staff supplied with the very finest and newest of instruments for dealing with the mass of correspondence which was constantly pouring through Army Headquarters.

Not the least important correspondents of the main General Staff were the Corps Staffs which were situated nearer to the firing line, and these in turn were fed by the Divisional Staffs who received their reports from the Brigade Majors, who in turn relied upon regimental reports. In addition to these sources of information, General Headquarters must necessarily keep in close touch with all that was happening at the French and Belgian Headquarters, for only by the closest co-operation could a successful defensive be maintained.

The offensive in Flanders, as already stated, now rested with the Allies, and it was on December 14, 1914, that fresh activities commenced and pressure was brought to bear along the whole line. Fierce conflicts were waged and violent struggles went on from day to day, entailing heavy losses on German and British alike. On one occasion the Indian troops suffered severely in a surprise attack made with great ferocity. The Guards also suffered the brunt of another attempt to carry a position. The same stubborn fighting was going on during December on the coast line. The Belgians were holding on with heroic patience and courage the line of the Yser. Holding Nieuport as they did, supported by the monitors and cruisers of the British fleet, they essayed again and again to advance toward Ostend.

Lombartzyde, a small village to the north of Nieuport, was shelled and taken first by the Belgians and then retaken by the Germans, and then yet again by the Belgians, until nothing was left but crumbling walls and hot ashes of what had once been a prosperous little community. The village of Westende suffered no better fate. Westende Bains, a beautiful plage upon the sea front, was wholly destroyed in order to get at the batteries of the enemy, which were sheltered behind.

It may be of interest to refer to what "Eye-Witness" calls the change that had come over what may be termed the "atmosphere" of the battlefield at this date. It had been one of the wettest Decembers on record, and everything had been made worse by the trying condition of the ground and the trenches. The floods were as embarrassing to our advance as they were to the enemy. Our soldiers were for days standing almost knee-deep in mud and water, often almost without shelter, against the pelting sleet and rain and the bursting shrapnel. The marshy nature of the soil intensified the discomfort; altogether it bore a grim aspect, this trial of heroic endurance, more especially during an advance or retreat, when there was little protection against the enemy's fire. During the long watches our soldiers endured the terrible hardships in their deep ditches and trenches of vile mud and rainwater with remarkable composure.

"Eye-Witness" described the conditions where the combatants were entrenched thus:

The cannonade has now decreased to such an extent that for hours on end nothing is heard but the frequent boom of one of the Allies' heavy guns, the occasional rattle of machine guns, and the intermittent "pop "—for that word expresses the sound best—of the snipers of either side.
And in certain quarters, where the combatants are close and operations appertain to those of siege warfare, the bombs of the Minenwerfer and the smaller bombs thrown by hand are detonating almost continuously.

But the air no longer throbs to the continuously dull roar of heavy artillery and the detonations of great projectiles. Of course, if an attack is in progress, there is again turmoil, but it is more local, and does not approach in intensity that which recently reigned on a large scale.

The scene, as a whole, as viewed from one of the few commanding points in our front, is almost one of peace as compared with that of a week or two ago. The columns of black smoke vomited by the exploding howitzer shell are as rare as those from burning villages.

The only generally visible signs of war are the occasional puffs of bursting shrapnel opening out above woods and villages and floating slowly away on the still air.

It was mentioned in the account of the fighting on the Aisne that so far as we were concerned the struggle had to some extent assumed the character of siege operations. The same can be said with still greater truth of the battle in which we are now engaged.

Both sides have had time to dig themselves in and to strengthen their positions with all the resources available in the field.

In spite of this the Germans, urged by weighty motives, limited as to time, and confident in their numerical superiority and the weight of a very powerful siege armament—such as has indeed never before been brought into the field— have when face to face with the Allies' line attempted to break it by frontal attacks.

Having failed in this, in spite of desperate efforts, they are now endeavouring in some quarters to progress by the slower methods of siege warfare. Until recently they have attempted to gain ground by assaulting our position across the open, seizing what they can of it, retaining and strengthening that and using it as a starting point for a fresh assault.
Their aim is still the same—to gain ground and drive us back—but owing to the immense loss entailed in the summary method of assaulting across the open for any distance the means employed are modified.

When bombardment is or has been severe everyone within range of the enemy's guns, the brigadier not excepted, will be found ensconced underground in "dug- outs" or "funk-holes," as they are familiarly called, for in the zone under fire houses are no better than shell traps.

Behind the firing line trenches are found the shelters for the men holding the line and those for the supports. These are more elaborate and comfortable than the fire trenches, usually are roofed over, and contain cooking places and many conveniences.

For some time the character of the artillery fire has been such as to force both combatants even for some distance behind the firing line to burrow into the earth in order to obtain shelter and to conceal their works as far as possible in order to gain protection both from guns and aeroplanes. This has been carried on to such an extent that behind the front fire trenches of British, French, and Germans are perfect labyrinths of burrows of various types. The principal feature of the battlefield, therefore, as has often been pointed out, is the absence of any signs of human beings.

Most of this trench fighting takes place at such close range that the guns of either side cannot fire at the enemy's infantry without great risk of hitting its own men. The rôle of artillery projectiles, however, is well played by bombs of all descriptions, which are used in prodigious quantities.

The larger ones projected by the Minenwerfer, of which the Germans employ three sizes, correspond to the heavy howitzer shells of the distant combat, and have much the same effect. They have a distinctive nickname of their own, but they may be termed the "Jack Johnsons" of the close attack of siege warfare.

The smaller bombs or grenades are thrown by hand from a few yards' distance, perhaps just lobbed over a parapet.

They are charged with high explosive and detonate with great violence; and since their impetus does not cause them to bury themselves in the earth before they detonate, their action, though local, is very unpleasant in the enclosed space between two traverses in a trench.
These grenades of various types are being thrown continuously by both sides, every assault being preluded and accompanied by showers of them. In fact, the wholesale use of these murderous missiles is one of the most prominent features of the close attack now being carried on.

As may be imagined, what with sharpshooters, machine guns and bombs, this kind of fighting is very deadly, and somewhat blind, owing to the difficulty of observation.

CHAPTER II — THE ATTEMPT TO BREAK THE BRITISH LINE

Reviewing the situation after six months of war, it could not be doubted that Germany was feeling the pinch in her great struggle. In the West and the East she was firmly held, and in the West each day was adding to the strength of the Allied line, though General Joffre, patient and careful, was content to wait his time.

At home Germany was displaying significant foresight. The Federal Council was empowered to take over the entire stock of bread cereals; all the grain and flour of the German Empire were to pass into possession of the State. In plain English, Germany was hoarding her food supplies, and taking steps to put her population on rations.

The relentless pressure of our sea-power had all but cut her off from the world. She had suffered enormous losses upon her huge battle-fronts. The great effort essential to German success had so far been foiled; it was estimated that Germany had lost two and a quarter millions of her best soldiers, and that her fresh efforts would have necessarily to be made with greatly inferior and disheartened troops.

It became more and more evident that this tremendous loss in men, combined with the failure of countless attacks that had been attempted in France and Flanders, had its effect on the moral of the enemy. Practically every attempt of the enemy at an offensive during the four long months that the rival forces had faced each other in the trenches had proved at best ineffective, at the worst a costly failure.

The official "Eye-Witness" commented on the mental and physical change which had come over the German soldiers. There did appear, he wrote in the middle of January, a difference in the state of feeling of the German rank and file from that which existed some weeks previous. Prisoners now seemed to realise that a victorious advance was out of the question, and that all that they could expect was to hold their ground. The immense sacrifices the enemy had made had proved to be without avail, and the weary, nerve-racked regiments were beginning to realise it. As regards physical well-being the German troops were not so favourably circumstanced as our own. They were less warmly clad, their medical arrangements were much inferior, and the conditions of the trenches in the trying weather were deplorable. Nevertheless, they showed the greatest bravery, and it almost seemed that the rank and file of the army were not backward in their efforts to support the overwhelming ambitions of the Prussian military caste and their vainglorious Kaiser.

Other signs of the impaired moral of the Germans were the extraordinary outburst of hatred against Great Britain and the despairing methods of warfare Germany began to adopt. There could be no doubt that at the end of six months of war a consciousness of ultimate impotence was beginning to come home to her. She was beginning to realise that her failure to end the war in less than six months, as she had fondly anticipated, was due to her plans being impossible of realisation. What was weighing heavily on the hearts of Germans was the sense of lost opportunity. They were face to face with tactical failure. There was now no question of Paris, of Calais, or of Warsaw. There was nothing but deadlock. And all this after the mighty efforts they had made, the vast losses they had suffered—losses which they had been prepared to make to attain success.

While they were being firmly held everywhere, and every attempt at offensive frustrated, they could not but realise that while they must grow weaker and weaker, the Allies would grow in strength from day to day. Germany alone, amongst all the belligerents, had prepared and was ready for war. She was equipped with men and guns to the highest point of possibility. And now, after six months, although she had still probably a preponderance of men in the field, it was certain, with the French reserves in readiness, and the great new Kitchener Army almost ready to take their place in the fighting line, that the conditions would be equalised, nay, reversed. Not only would the Allies have a greater number of men and a preponderance in artillery, but the advantage in moral superiority. And it must be remembered that all the while Germany continued to lose more men than the Allies in the trench warfare. Their method was nearly always the same. They sent forward wave after wave of men, the invariable result being losses out of all proportion to any advantage gained. Sometimes the great pressure of men they threw forward resulted in their overwhelming the defenders and occupying the trenches temporarily. The vigorous counter-attacks of the Allies resulted in their winning back the ground which might have been lost. There were enormous losses on both sides, but the disadvantage was always on the side of the enemy. This kind of warfare was one of attrition and the Allies were well able to stand the test.

In the Caucasus, the enemy's newest ally, Turkey, had been soundly trounced by the Russians, and in Egypt we had beaten off the invading Turkish army. In the west, everywhere, our Allies were confident that it was well-nigh impossible for Germany to score any decisive success. A French official account of the progress of operations summed up the position thus:

"It can then be affirmed that, in order to obtain a complete success, France and her Allies have only to wait and prepare for it with untiring patience. The offensive power of the Allies, constantly reinforcing their Armies in strength, officers and supplies, is daily increasing, and it is therefore to their interest to make their maximum effort at the moment when they will have at their disposition the maximum of means. This is what they will do; all that matters is to achieve a complete result without useless sacrifices."

Also—and this was another factor of great importance—the artillery of the Allies was slowly acquiring an equality with the artillery of the Germans. It had been the other way in the beginning, but now nearly every conflict of the guns showed things to be otherwise. In successive days of one week of fierce artillery duels, when the German expended twice as many projectiles as his opponent, the big French guns achieved marked successes. On one day they destroyed two enemy guns; on the next they demolished two batteries and silenced another; the day after they accounted for a battery of 15-centimetre guns; and on the fourth day, near Béthencourt (this illuminating little record covers only a small section of the four hundred mile line), they destroyed two batteries of 77-millimetre guns. Equal in effectiveness was the work of the British artillery. In more than once place, too, it was found that the German shells were ineffective, and did not burst well. Over all the western battlefield, as we left the old year behind and came, full of hope, into the New Year, the success of our artillery was established.

To this brief summary of how things stood there should be added a last word. The British and French airmen, by their initiative and daring, had secured the whip-hand in the air. Capable and cool, temperamentally more adventurous than their adversaries, the flying man of the Allies proved himself continually more than a match for his enemy.
Every day there were instances of the courage and resource of our men, for hardly a day passed, whatever the conditions, that British and French airmen did not ascend. On more than one occasion our airmen carried out observations not more than a thousand feet above the enemy's trenches. British airmen threw bombs on the enemy's aviation camp at Linselles, and paid several marauding visits to Ostend, both by night and day. Only when the weather was clear and calm did they encounter enemy machines, and not infrequently the Germans fled at their approach. Very often the former would make a half turn immediately they perceived their more daring adversaries, but it was not often that a combat took place; when it did, almost invariably the French or British airmen came off victorious.

A fine example of an aerial flight was supplied by an exploit of one of the French aviators in the region of Cernay. In the course of a reconnaissance the Frenchman gave chase to a German opponent and twice obliged him to make a half turn, thus preventing him from flying over the Allies' lines.

The moment the German reached the safety of his own lines the Frenchman perceived another German aeroplane going towards Belfort and immediately gave chase. He soon came within range of the German and opened a lively fusillade, which was returned and kept up for a distance of 150 metres until they reached the environs of Mulhouse, where the German was compelled to descend before he was able to reach his own sheds.

In the course of reconnaissances, the Allied airmen often experienced a fusillade from the guns of the enemy. The machines were on some occasions pierced by shot and by the bursting of shells, but the sang-froid of the pilots enabled them to return safely, sometimes under the most perilous conditions. One airman, in consequence of a mishap to his engine, was obliged to cross the enemy's lines at a height of 150 metres in the region of Hartmannsweilerkopf, which is very hilly. In spite of a fierce fire directed at him when crossing a wooded part, the airman gained the valley of the Thur and descended in the French lines safe and sound.

"Eye-Witness" gave us some interesting details about the work of aerial reconnaissance. The observer either travels above a previously selected line of country, or passes to and fro over a certain area, recording everything of value that he sees. This latter method is the slower, and is used only when very detailed information is required.

This is not work which can be carried out by everyone. The really first-rate observer must possess extensive military knowledge in order to know what objects to look for and where to look for them; he must have very good eyesight in order to pick them up, and he must have a knack of reading a map quickly both in order to mark correctly their positions and to find his way. To reconnoitre is not easy even in fine weather; but in driving rain or snow, in a temperature perhaps several degrees below zero, or in a gale, when an aeroplane travelling with the wind rocks and sways like a ship in a heavy sea, and may attain a speed of 150 miles an hour, the difficulties are immense.

In these circumstances, and from the altitude at which it is necessary to fly in order to escape the projectiles of anti-aircraft guns, columns of transport or of men are easily missed. Indeed, at a first attempt an observer will see nothing which is of military value, for it is only after considerable practice that the eye becomes accustomed to scouring a great stretch of country from above, and acquires the power of distinguishing objects upon it.

Psychology also comes in, and the temperament of an observer is of the greatest importance. He must be cool and capable of great concentration in order to keep his attention fixed upon his objective in spite of all distractions, such as, for instance, the bursts of shell close to him, or the noise of rifle bullets passing through the planes of his machine. He must withstand the temptation to make conjectures, or to think that he has seen something when he is not absolutely certain of the fact, since an error in observing or an inaccuracy in reporting may lead to false conclusions and cause infinite harm.

Many men are absolutely unfitted for such duty, and even trained observers, observed "Eye-Witness," vary in their powers of reconnaissance.

January 27th was the Kaiser's birthday. It was generally expected that to mark this event the Germans would attempt to gain something that would have the appearance of a signal victory. Not only would a German offensive success have been a pleasant offering on the part of the Army to the Kaiser to celebrate his fifty-sixth birthday, but it would have had much more important results if it had succeeded in heartening Berlin, where the population was beginning to be doubtful and dispirited.

So the days immediately preceding the War Lord's birthday saw violent efforts by the enemy to secure a decisive victory at various points.

The Kaiser himself came to the German Headquarters in France, and made a tour of the positions of his troops in the region of La Bassée, where very large forces had been concentrated, obviously with the set purpose of a desperate offensive movement. The presence of the Kaiser indicated clearly enough the importance the enemy attached to this projected effort. The first of the birthday honours, therefore, was to be sought for here, in the region of La Bassée and Festubert, where many sanguinary battles had been fought during these last months.

The Emperor had been the witness of what the Germans called the "great Success" at Soissons (where, owing to the flooding of the Aisne which broke the communicating bridges, the French had been obliged to retire), and doubtless the commanders of the Northern armies, anxious that all the honour of visible achievements should not fall upon von Kluck's army, were desirous of making a show which should earn for them the same amount of praise as had fallen to the commander of the German forces, which, as already stated, by reason of the rapidly rising floods of the Aisne, had been able to push the French troops back across the river.

About two miles from La Bassée was Festubert, a name which will be associated in the minds of soldiers for many years to come with one of the most bloody and relentless battles in which the British have been engaged. About Givenchy for months had ebbed and flowed the tide of battle. Even as the Allies had as their objective La Bassée, with its command of the road to Lille, so had the German, in all the efforts he has made, directed his attention to a town of corresponding importance—the town of Bethune, on the direct road to Boulogne, Calais, and the coast.

The British line concerned in the birthday attack ran from Richebourg through Festubert, Givenchy, to Cuinchy. This line therefore straddled the railway between Bethune and La Bassée, and also ran astride the La Bassée canal, which flows within a few yards of and parallel to the railway. From the first, although the attack was first delivered upon Cuinchy, it was evident that the German's objective was the village of Givenchy. There was reason enough, from the strategical standpoint. Givenchy, a mining and industrial village, stands upon rising ground amidst a veritable dessert of mud, across which it is almost impossible to move infantry and quite impossible to transport guns. Commanding, as it does, the La Bassée road, and giving on to Bethune, the possession of Givenchy was a matter of the first importance, and even as the British had made considerable sacrifices to hold it and had driven back attack after attack delivered against its defences, so did the German consider it worth while to make even greater sacrifices in order to secure this position.

It was eight o'clock in the morning when, without any warning, the first lines of German troops suddenly emerged from their trenches and came sweeping across the sodden area "in waves," and secured, after desperate fighting, the first line of British trenches.

It was a grey day. A slight mist covered the distant plains. The British troops were at breakfast when the first serious warning came to them that an attack in force was being developed. Immediately the men in the trenches stood to arms, and firing steadily with rifle and machine gun they cleared line after line of the attacker from their front, only to find that the dead men were replaced by others, who pressed forward shoulder to shoulder, and, swamping the opposition by sheer weight of numbers, poured into the trenches, which were only evacuated just in time.

The 56th Prussian Regiment, which bore the brunt of the attack, pressed on to the very outskirts of the village itself, and was there met and decimated by an appalling fire from trench and housetop and window. None the less the German held on, seizing every cover, wall, and house. Every mean little house in the village of Givenchy had been converted into a fortress, and one British regiment in particular—the Gloucesters—offered a desperate resistance. It seemed for a while as though the Germans had succeeded. They had driven the British back until there stretched between the lines of the lost trenches and the German advance guard 300 yards of holding mud, which could only be crossed under heavy fire with the certainty of enormous loss.

The attack had been sudden, almost unexpected in such strength, and comparatively small as was the British force that confronted the horde now bringing a portion of its reserves into line, it seemed likely that the German would consolidate his position. The British had lost their first line of trenches outside the village. They now lost a number of trenches which were closer to the village itself, and the 56th Prussians and some Pioneers were working gallantly to establish themselves in the village itself. The British regiments were on their mettle, and the commander of the forces in that sector, alive to all the dangers and to all the possibilities which the occupation of Givenchy entailed, was moving his reinforcements.

And now the French to the south were taking a hand. On narrow country roads the transports and the ambulance, and all the impedimenta which weave to and fro between the base and the advance lines, were moving to the side of the road at a warning shout, even as London drivers will seek the kerb when the clang of a fire-engine bell sounds its warning.

In the clear space in the middle of the road, broken by wear and sodden with incessant rain, battery after battery of French 75's dashed past, their whips cracking, the steel hooves of their horses striking fire from the flint pavé. They were flying along to take up a position which would offer the British support. Gun after gun, swaying and slithering through the mud, came into action, and to the deeper tone of the British batteries at Festubert, firing desperately at the advancing host of the enemy's reserves, were added the sharper crash of the 75 and the dull roar of its explosive shell. Eventually the guns hammered back the German supports and gave a breathing space to the battling British in the grim village of Givenchy.

Givenchy was a shambles. From every window fire belched down upon the advancing German. Helmeted men, white-faced and bleeding, staggered to the protection of walls, instantly shattered by the shells of the British artillery, which was now firing at short range. The scream and whistle of flying projectiles, the incessant and deadly rattle of machine-gun fire, the swift exchange of shells, the crash of the bursting grenades—all these combined to furnish a complete pandemonium which left even experienced soldiers dazed and bewildered.

A number of Germans at one end of the village succeeded in holding houses, and when the British poured back, these little dwellings became the scene of those silent bayonet fights which have been a remarkable feature of the war.

Into one of these houses, held by eight Germans, went a British soldier, such as Kipling loves to draw. A short, discoloured clay pipe held all the time in the corner of his mouth, a rifle and bayonet in his strong hands, he fought off their combined attack, bayoneted four and took the other four prisoners.

So close was the fighting in these houses and in the small confines of the apartments which ordinarily the miner of the district occupies, that often there was no room even for bayonet play, and men went to work with their fists, battering and beating their enemy to submission, or using their bayonets as knives, and fighting hand-to-hand. The British were irresistible. They swept the village clear of the enemy, and from the vantage place of the houses they poured such a terrible fire into their old trenches close to the village (the Germans had occupied these) that all who did not die under that terrible onslaught were glad to surrender.

The end of the fight was not yet. Driven from the village, shot out of the trenches, the Germans came back again to the attack, not once, but in all five times, before the violence of the assault was shattered. In the brick-fields which lay about Givenchy there was a chaos of fighting, over a battle-ground of mud so deep in places as to be a morass.

Friend and foe were mixed up in little struggling knots. Over the German reserve shells were bursting in increasing quantity.

The French 75's in the south, the British heavy guns at Festubert in the north, concentrated their fire upon the thick grey masses, which lay waiting the opportunity and the means of throwing their weight into the scale.

There was no way up to the village across the plain. This was no more than a quagmire, into which men sank to their knees and often to their necks. It was the La Bassée road or nothing, and upon the La Bassée road every British gun was concentrated. It mattered not to them that, farther to the east, the heavy German batteries had come into action and were sending their shrieking messengers of death towards the French and British artillery positions. Undaunted, undismayed, when bursting shell wrecked and scattered gun and limber, the artillery stuck to their work, pumping fire upon the road up which the German supports vainly endeavoured to move, and only relaxing their attention to this road when it became necessary to silence a too venturesome German battery which had exposed itself beyond the safety point.

The retirement of the British before Givenchy had forced the French line farther south, to bend back in sympathy. At Vermelles, gained at such sacrifice, the French held on. At Festubert in the north the British line was hardly affected.

The first attack had developed before Cuinchy, and this was merely the prelude to the more serious attack upon the main position. In the struggle which ended in the final victory of the British, many are the stories of individual heroism and of splendid courage in the face of extraordinary and terrifying circumstances. One soldier, who was caught in the trenches at Cuinchy and was unable to make his escape before the avalanche of German infantry poured into the trench, succeeded, in spite of an occasional bayonet prod from the enemy, in shamming dead during all the time they occupied the British trench. When they flowed out to their final attack upon the village, leaving the empty trench untenanted, as they thought, save for the bodies of their dead comrades, this man opened a brisk fire into the backs of the advancing Germans and fought off a patrol which was sent back to dispose of him. A British armoured train, moving westward at the first hint of the attack, brought its naval guns into action, and added to the din of bombardment to which the German was subjected.

For three hours the fate of the British 1st Division in that sector hung in the balance. Not only the fate of the British integrity line, but the conformation of the whole of the Allies' line from the Lys to the Somme was largely dependent upon the superhuman efforts of the British. In this region, on a previous occasion, the German masses had succeeded in driving the Indians from their trenches, which were only regained after bloody fighting. It was at Givenchy and Festubert that our men had, once before, fought their way forward, house by house, and succeeded in pushing back the Germans. As they had succeeded then, so they succeeded now.

The British had therefore a painful knowledge of the difficulties to be overcome in this part of the field, and so far profited by the lessons which earlier fighting had taught them that they did not give an inch of ground away which was not necessary. At eleven o'clock in the morning the German attack had reached its zenith, and it was now evident to the British commander that he had no reason to fear that a complete occupation of his position would follow the German attack. His supports and his reinforcements were being hurried forward. Bethune was sending out long columns of troops. Reserves, including the London Scottish, were following these.

At one o'clock the British commander had the position so well in hand that he decided upon his counter-attack.

Five violent attacks had been made by the German before he established himself on the outskirts of Givenchy. One single attack, steady, persistent and relentless, drove him back to his trenches, and placed the British, not, it is true, in the position which they had occupied in the morning and which had been rendered untenable and had broken up by their own shell fire, but in a new line of trenches only a very short distance behind these.

Knee-deep through mud and water and quicksand, the British ploughed back slowly, unconcerned by the fury of the fire which the German was now directing towards him. As the British advanced towards Cuinchy, so did the French on our right move forward to re-occupy the line, from which they had not indeed been driven. They had voluntarily sacrificed it in order that their front should conform the more closely with ours.

The German, in his advance, as in his retirement, had been handicapped by the fact that along the main line of his movement towards his objective ran the length of La Bassée canal, so that his forces were separated by this waterway, and were so acting independently one of the other. Caught by our machine-guns upon this stretch of road, the Germans to the south of the canal suffered perhaps even more severely than those who had been engaged in the abortive attempt to carry Givenchy by assault.

Such was the outcome of the most important effort to signalise the Kaiser's birthday. Another and also a very desperate effort was made at Ypres.

Against Ypres, battered and bruised, scarred and maimed by enemy shells, the full force of the German reserves in Flanders was mustered, and a grand attack was commenced on January 25th. This was no new ground to the German. He had made since the beginning of the trench war a succession of violent assaults upon this position; he had sent his Prussian Guards and his overwhelming divisions to swamp the remnant of the 7th British Division, which, hastily entrenched before that town, had succeeded in throwing back an enemy five times his strength.

If he had failed against that attenuated line, he was less likely to succeed now when the trenches before and to the north of Ypres were held thickly by some of the best regiments in the French Army, supported by their deadly 75's. Nevertheless, such was the inspiring influence of the highest War Lord that the attempt was made, and great masses of troops were brought up, and in the early morning the inevitable artillery pounding began. Every piece that could be brought into play was directed towards the French trenches. Howitzers, "coal- boxes," field guns, mines, mortars, and the whole arsenal of German artillery began this furious and nerve-racking bombardment. This lasted for an hour, at the end of which time the position was considered to be prepared for immediate attack; the grey lines of German infantry, scrambling from their trenches and supported by masses of reserves, came straight for the French defences.

In describing this battle, the writer of the French communiqué used a phrase which, by its very vividness and because of the picture it conveys, is at once arresting and ineffaceable. He said, "The attack was stopped dead." In this brief sentence is told the story of the German failure.

Met by concentrated rifle and machine-gun fire of extraordinary ferocity and fury, the Kaiser's legions melted away long before they were near enough to deliver their attack by bayonet, and after a painful period of hesitation, broke and retired, leaving the ground before the French line covered with dead. Thus this other attempt at a birthday honour ended in disaster.

There was still more to come.

Not unmindful of the significance of the day, the British greeted the dawn of the 27th with a shower of lyddite shells, directed against a house near the village of Messines, which had been marked down by the British commander for early destruction. This house had evidently been used as a store for hand grenades and for artillery ammunition, for the explosion of the "birthday shells" against this house was followed by a succession of minor explosions as the bombs in the store went off, and this appropriate display of fireworks represented the final British contribution to the festivities of the Emperor's natal day.

CHAPTER III — THE TAKING OF NEUVE CHAPELLE

I have already dealt with the situation at the end of six months of war. Lord Kitchener told us in a speech in the House of Lords that the water-logged state of the trenches, combined with bad weather, had necessarily restricted the work of the army to trench warfare. For several weeks more a period of seeming inaction prevailed.

The brief bulletins had little to tell; one day a trench was captured, the next another was successfully mined. A day later a gain of 100 yards or so might be recorded, and occasionally the communique informed us frankly that there was "nothing to report." In Flanders in particular, this was the condition of things throughout February. Notwithstanding, the men were ready and eager to move. What were the British doing before La Bassée and in the neighbourhood of Ypres? So far as the German knew—nothing. Such of his daring scouts as crossed the area saw little to arouse the apprehension of the most timid of commanders.

Had they travelled by night, with means to pierce the darkness, they would have seen long ammunition trains moving swiftly from the coast, along roads which were kept clear; they would have seen battery after battery of artillery moving across country; they would have watched great naval guns and howitzer batteries being established in their places.

The nights were full of feverish activity. Sweating men in their shirt- sleeves, despite the cold, worked at top speed, loading and unloading shells, whilst thousands of motor-wagons came swiftly through the night to various points, deposited their deadly loads and went back again. Well in the rear the field batteries were putting the final touch to gun and harness. Somewhere in the rear, too, the reserve corps were making very careful preparations for the struggle ahead.

On March 8, when the Champagne battle was reaching its critical point, the British showed their hand. South of Ypres, from the village of St. Éloi and along that section of the line which runs south past Armentières, they began a cannonading of no unusual intensity, but serious enough to direct the attention of the German to this portion of the line. The German sent up support in anticipation of the inevitable assault, yet the events of that Monday took no more exciting shape than this intermittent and, for the British, strangely economical bombardment which went on all along his front.

There was also some evidence of activity in the region of Neuve Chapelle. Here, however, the German commander thought he detected nothing more serious than a very natural desire on the part of the commander of this section to engage the attention of the German left flank. Neuve Chapelle had been well organised for defence. It was a bastion thrust into the British lines, and had been the scene of terrible fighting, until the German on this section had asserted, by weight of numbers and heaviness of metal, his superiority over his enemy. Yet the British could not be wholly thrown back, had clung to the end of the village and waited, hungry-eyed, for the moment when they would again hold its walls. Obviously it could not be from here that danger threatened, and as that cannonading increased in vigour from Ypres and the southern line, the tendency of the German was shown in a general tightening up to confront attack from that quarter.

Monday and Tuesday, March 8 and 9, were thus passed with the thunder of guns rolling down the line, loudest from behind St. Éloi, and more feeble and tapering off to spasmodic explosions where the line curved inward to the westward of Neuve Chapelle and continued to Festubert and Givenchy. Wednesday, March 10, broke, a cloudy yet fairly pleasant morn, and it began, as usual, in the neighbourhood of Neuve Chapelle with a scattering exchange of shots between the outlying trenches and the steady "klik-klok" of the German snipers' rifles. On the enemy's side, as on the British side, the men went to their breakfast as though this day formed merely one in a seemingly endless routine of trench warfare.

"We had an extra ration of sausage that morning," said a German prisoner ruefully, "and our captain told us that there would be little to do, so we sat down to play a game of cards, leaving the usual number of look-out men to warn us of danger. I had a peep over the parapet. I could see a blue curl of smoke rising from behind the British trenches, and I said to my friend: 'These Englanders have their breakfast very late.' The scene was quite peaceful, though very sad."

It was to be less peaceful and a great deal more sad for the German Army that day. Somewhere between half-past seven and eight o'clock in the morning a single gun from the British lines crashed, and a shrapnel shell came shrieking overhead, to burst before the very centre of the main German trench. It was followed at an interval by the boom of a heavy gun in the distance. The shell fell a little short. There was a long interval and then another boom, and the shriek of an oncoming shell; this time it fell beyond the trench. Again there was a pause, and then the third heavy shell burst, this time at the exact distance before the trench, blowing in the trench and killing half-a-dozen men.

There was just an interval of time to allow the unseen observer to signal back the result of a shot, and then, in the language of a British officer, "hell broke loose." The whole of the British line seemed to burst of a sudden into flame. Flames leaped from farm and ridge, from hollow, from cover of wood, from sunken road, from hedge, parapet and fieldwork. It was a flare of fire fringing a hundred trenches; it was a fire which came bubbling impatiently from machine- gun batteries, and the German infantrymen, crouching in their trenches terrified, counted the shells bursting in their immediate vicinity and found they averaged one in every ten seconds.

Rising to a climax this bombardment by 150 guns became appalling. The shrieking of the shells in the air, their explosion and the continuous thunder of the batteries all merged into one great volume of sound. The discharge of the guns was so rapid that they sounded like the fire of gigantic machine gun. During the 35 minutes it continued our men could show themselves freely and even walk about in perfect safety. German prisoners also confessed that they had never experienced such a bombardment as that which preceded the assault on Neuve Chapelle.

One wounded Prussian officer of a particularly offensive and truculent type, which is not uncommon, expressed the greatest contempt for this method of bombarding. "You do not fight. You murder," he said: "If it had been straightforward honest fighting we should have beaten you; but we never had a chance from the first. There was a shell every ten yards. Nothing could live in such a fire."

This feeling of resentment against our artillery, according to the official "Eye-Witness," was shown by several of the prisoners. "Gratifying as it is to our gunners, it is an exhibition of a curious lack of any judicial sense or even of a rudimentary sense of humour on the part of the apostles of frightfulness." It was the Germans who prepared an overwhelming force of artillery before the war, and they were the first to apply the concentrated action of heavy guns in field warfare. When the tables are turned and they have their first taste of what we have often eaten they actually have the effrontery to complain.

During the terrific bombardment the fire from the German trenches entirely ceased. The men dared not come over the parapet for fear of the consequences. They crouched in the bottom with commendable caution, listening open-eyed to the frantic pandemonium. Those of them who were seen immediately after the battle were hypnotised—half mad with terror and frenzy. It is said that there were no fewer than 150 guns working at top speed during this terrific onslaught.

"The earth shook as though there was a storm," said an Indian officer watching this display. "It was as if the mountains were sliding and monsters were struggling in the earth."

The Indians held one section of the British trenches. They had not lost their dart despite the terrible hardships which a winter campaign entailed upon men who were born and bred in a torrid clime. They waited as impatiently as any for the word "Go!" and presently the firing ceased and the signal for attack was given. Over the ground, unswept by rifle fire as yet—for the enemy were still shaken and dazed with terror and did not realise that the bombardment had ceased—there swept a giant wave of khaki, bristling with bayonets; wave after wave of men surged forward crashing through the barbed wire into the first line of trenches. Here the fight was short. Upraised hands and ashen faces told the story of the terrific bombardment to which they had previously been subjected.

"Our men checked to kill," said an observer, "and went on."

In less than half-an-hour almost the whole elaborate series of German trenches was in our hands. Except at one point there was little resistance, for the trenches, which in places were literally blotted out, were filled with dead and dying, buried in earth and debris, and the majority of the survivors were in no mood for further fighting.

In an extraordinarily short space of time the village of Neuve Chapelle, which the enemy had held since the end of October, was taken. The grimy gunners, watching from their positions, saw the infantrymen swamp the advance trenches, heard the crackle of rifle fire in the village itself, and knew that they had done their work well. The village was in our hands. We were beyond the church tower, that landmark, and save at one point had swept the environs free of the enemy. That one point, which resisted with desperate gallantry, was locally known as "Port Arthur"; and it was a strongly organised defensive position which defied for a time every effort the British made to take it. Finally, at half-past five in the afternoon the men in khaki, not to be denied, carried this last stronghold at the point of the bayonet.

The British corps had encircled Neuve Chapelle, and Germans, fighting in the street—and fighting with great gallantry—retired only to find their exit blocked by masses of British troops which had come round on the outskirts of the village and were now holding the outlet. A great number of Germans surrendered, and thousands were killed during the day. Nevertheless, the British had to meet two vigorous counter-attacks, for now the railway lines in the rear of the German front were working at top pressure, reserves pouring into the German line, and large numbers of the men who had been concentrated near Ypres were brought down post-haste to stiffen the shattered regiments.

By nightfall we were in possession of all the enemy's trenches, on a front of 4,000 yards, representing an advance of more than 1,200 yards from our original trenches at the furthest point. This was on Wednesday, the 10th, and throughout that night and on the following morning the fighting continued. Along the whole front around the village and to the north of it, the German delivered attack after attack. "Men fell in swathes," said a witness. "Whole companies melted away before the British machine-gun fire and before the heavy artillery firing which met them sometimes at point-blank range."

Far away to the right, the French, not to be debarred from participation, brought their artillery into action, covered the road up which reinforcements must pass, shelled the enemy convoys and batteries as they moved to the front, and rendered that splendid assistance which we have always expected from our brave Ally and have invariably received. The German effort was grimly determined. On one part of the line they gained a trench, but were immediately surrounded and the whole of the occupants were captured. The British gave the enemy no rest. Sweeping out beyond the village, they captured a mill, and such was the exhaustion of the German troops that here as elsewhere whole companies surrendered. The Germans had fought a gallant fight. The village itself was a shambles, thickly covered with the dead of attacker and defender, and men were found who had gone completely mad under the strain of bombardment. This may explain some of the atrocious deeds which the enemy committed—the stabbing of a Royal Army Medical Corps man whilst he was bandaging a wounded German; the shooting of British wounded which an officer described, and which he said was but one of a hundred instances; and the ferocity of the counter-attacks which were delivered again and again, but always unsuccessfully, against the British lines.

"By nightfall," wrote the official Eye-Witness, "the German dead lay thick all along the front. Opposite the sector south of the village there were more than 2,000 bodies; and in front of one battalion east of the village stretched 500 more. The ground in these places sloped upwards from our trenches towards the enemy, and the corpses could be plainly seen and counted. These figures do not include the large number killed in the village of Neuve Chapelle itself— where many bodies lay buried amongst the ruins and hidden among the fallen masonry—nor behind the line occupied by us."

The night of the 12th passed more or less quietly, and at dawn on the 13th there was a repetition of the German tactics, great masses of infantry being put to the British position, only to be swept away by machine-gun and rifle fire. To the east of the village of Neuve Chapelle is a little wood known as the Bois du Biez, one of those abrupt plantations partaking of the nature of a very large copse, very useful to a belligerent for concealing the movements of troops and for screening from observation his gun positions. It served him in this case since he was able to concentrate new reserves and debouch them on to the British line. Here, however, his purpose was foiled by a concentration of fire which first checked, then stopped, and finally drove the supports back in disorderly confusion. Again the British gunners came to the rescue and swept one small area clear, that area being the ground over which the German reserves were passing or must pass.

"The artillery were dropping the shells just where they wanted them," said one of our officers. "It was as though they were at target practice, and each battery was competing for a prize. An artillery observer who was standing by me said that no fewer than six batteries were all dropping shells in an area represented by a circle with a diameter of 20 yards!"

Yet the Germans were continuing in haste to send troops forward. The railways behind their front were kept busy day and night. The little town of Don, which is an important railway junction from a strategical point of view, was the scene of the greatest activity in this region; but if the German general was to depend upon the troops which came through this small nodal point, he was to receive a shock, for British airmen came swiftly from the skies, dropped their high explosive bombs on the station and completely wrecked the junction. It is possible that it was here that the German general who had control of the whole of the railway organisation in the West was killed. A similar attack was made upon the junction at Douai, with excellent results.

Saturday the 13th, saw the British in firm occupation of the village of Neuve Chapelle. Where the line had sagged it now bulged, and we may suppose that on their newly gained ground the British artillery was making new gun positions, for from here it was possible to shell one of the communications leading to La Bassée.

On Sunday the attacks ceased, The German general had realised the impossibility of pushing the British back from Neuve Chapelle, and he must devise a method by which he could bring about a sympathetic retirement, without again facing those awful defences which had been created in a night before the ruined village. Mention has already been made of a concentration of troops somewhere in the neighbourhood of St. Éloi. Undoubtedly a portion of these were employed in some of the counter-attacks upon Neuve Chapelle.

There was, at any rate, a large force available for employment on the St. Éloi front; and on the Sunday morning the German, imitating the tactics of the British, opened a furious bombardment upon our troops defending this village and delivered a surprise attack, blowing in the first line of trenches and driving the defenders to the western end of St. Éloi. This occurred just before dark, and the German general hoped, by reaching his new position before darkness set in, to utilise the friendly cover of the night to organise a defence which would prevent the British retaking the ground without weakening the line before Neuve Chapelle. If he imagined that a night attack held any terror for the British, who are the designers of night attacks, he had learned little from our military history and nothing at all from the war.

At three o'clock in the morning the British counter-attack was organised and dispatched. The night was misty, and the scene of the assault upon the village was one of the most picturesque that had been seen on the Western side. By the light of blazing houses great columns of men emerged from the darkness and flung themselves upon the barricades which the Germans had erected in the streets of St. Éloi itself. By daylight our men had retaken all they had lost, and the grey of dawn broke upon this terrible little village where dead men lay in every conceivable position, and where the dull, red glow of burning buildings spoke eloquently of that awful night's work.

The British had retaken the village; they had re-occupied most of the trenches to the east of the village, and all those that were not re-occupied by us were either broken up or untenanted by the enemy. This German attack, which was delivered in considerable force and was designed to throw back the British line to where it had been before they advanced through Neuve Chapelle, had proved a costly failure.

Altogether the German losses in four days' fighting were estimated at 18,000.

CHAPTER IV — THE FIGHT FOR HILL 60

The battle of Neuve Chapelle, heroic and decisive as it was, could not be regarded as anything more than an important local success; just as the battle of Soissons in February, proclaimed as a great victory by the Germans, was but a local defeat of the French.

The affair of Neuve Chapelle was a battle on a big scale, and in any previous war it would have proved something of a decisive event with far-reaching results. But now, so enormous was the field of operations and the number of combatants engaged, that beyond demonstrating the increased power of our artillery and the fervour and fighting spirit of our troops, beyond marking an advance of some two miles over a front of four miles, and wresting from the enemy a strongly fortified strategical position, our victory, as regards immediate results, was simply a local defeat for the Germans with the infliction of heavy losses. Nevertheless it might prove to be a landmark in the campaign, just as the battle of Ypres marked an epoch in the war.

The lull in the Carpathians decided the Kaiser's advisers. News came that all railway traffic between Belgium and Holland was to be held up; that the frontier was to be closed. And there trickled through to the neutral countries many rumours to the effect that large bodies of troops were being poured through the Rhine provinces into Belgium, and that in Western Germany all passenger traffic had been disorganised in consequence. This could only mean one thing. General Joffre and Field-Marshal French were not taken by surprise. In all probability they had news of the coming of these new forces long before the German gave the world a hint as to his intentions by closing the frontier. It was the expected effort—the effort anticipated in the early part of the year, and deferred because of the pressing engagement which the German Army had elsewhere.

Obviously, this new activity affected the British and the Belgians more than it did the French. Only a small portion of the French Army was in Flanders, holding the line which curved round from Nieuport to Ypres, and this portion was the connecting link between the Belgian and the British armies. The French force farther south would not feel the pressure of any new German formations for a considerable time.

Ypres lay on the way from Germany, and Ypres was one of those sentimental points of conquest which the German had set himself to secure. For months, battles had waged with intermittent violence along this sector. Indeed, ever since the gallant 7th Division had, with its attenuated line, held off attack after attack delivered by the flower of German infantry, silence had not reigned in this tragic area.

South of Ypres the German had established himself for a few hours, after Neuve Chapelle had been taken, in St. Éloi, only to be driven out from that village and back to his stronghold, which was marked on the map as Hill 60. Hill 60, lies to the south-east of the village of Zillebeke, which might be described as a suburb village of Ypres. In a country which is remarkable for its flatness, Hill 60, although it stands less than 200 feet high, was an important eminence, of great value to the enemy for purposes of artillery observation. It commanded a view of Menin, dominated the village of Gheluvelt to its left, and the two main roads from Ypres to Menin and from Menin to Roulers. The German had originally occupied "60 metre hill," after we had been forced to loose our hold upon Gheluvelt, the village which, the readers will remember, was the scene of such extraordinary house-to-house fighting, wherein the Worcester Regiment covered itself with glory.

Although little more than a gentle swell in the ground, as "Eye-Witness" told us, Hill 60 was the highest part of the ridge, and had formed the scene of desperate fighting in the past, British, German and French having all contested it.

Throughout November, December and January, this section of the Allied front was held by the French, and during that time the hill changed hands more than once, but the final result, when the line was again occupied by us in February, was that the German still held the crest.

For the British to take that Hill by assault, to advance across a mined plain, entrenched and swept by massed batteries of machine-guns, would have entailed greater sacrifice of life than had been experienced in any battle in which the British had been engaged during the war.

The German method of attack in such a case was the obvious method. But the German method is not that of the British. Against such a position the German would hurl massed troops. Shoulder to shoulder in close dense formation he would have sent his grey-coats and would have watched them melt away under the spraying fire of the Maxims, without remorse and without any doubt or hesitation.

"The British sacrifice material, but they do not sacrifice men," wrote a French officer. "If a motor-car does not fire properly they throw it away and use a new one. If a motor-cycle requires some repair they put it on the old iron heap and take a new one. If there is any doubt as to whether they ought to supply rations for 6,000 or 7,000, they supply rations for 10,000. But they are very jealous for their men, and do not know the word 'Kismet' where human lives are concerned. They say that money is nothing and that life is everything."

Hussar tactics are admirable. Dash and initiative and the high, hot courage of battle are to be commended. But there is another quality in war which counts more than any, and that is patience combined with perseverance.

The battle line had settled down to the conventional exchanges of shells and bullets. The British had established themselves on the outer edges of Neuve Chapelle and St. Éloi and had entrenched themselves more strongly than ever, maintaining their place in the line, and it seemed that after the heavy casualties which they had sustained in the two battles they were content to sit down waiting for the first move to come from the German.

Hill 60, looming up in the near distance, ringed with steel and fire, forbidding and menacing, confronted the irregular trench lines which the British occupied. Sniper shot at sniper; great guns, masked by the hill, sent their shrieking messengers of death at irregular intervals; but for long no evidence of unusual activity would have been observed on either side.

"From my look-out," wrote a friend to the present writer, "I see a zig-zag trench occupied by Tommies. At regular intervals in the trench there are watchers peering through the spy-hole in the steel plates which are provided to guard the observer. Four of the men are playing cards, two or three are grouped together in an animated discussion. They are dressed in all sorts of nondescript headgear, for the day is fairly cold, with slight showers of rain. Before the trench a few poor, weakling trees are standing. And a few, snapped in two by shell-fire as though broken across a giant's knee, lie across the trench and are used for fuel.

"To the right are the remains of what was once a prosperous farmhouse, and now consists of three walls, blackened with smoke; whilst in front of us is a triple line of barbed wire, against which a dead and bloated cow lies, her stiff legs pointing up into the air. Farther to the front are more remnants of houses, a few gaunt walls and a shattered church tower; whilst between that and our trench is an irregular scar in the earth. This is a German trench line.

"Overhead, sailing like a majestic bird, is an English biplane, pursued by a little puff of white smoke from the enemy anti-aircraft guns. But the pilot doesn't seem to bother, and when he might come down in perfect safety to our own lines, he turns his machine and goes sailing back the way he came, these spiteful little woolly balls bursting left, right, but always below him.

"He reminds me of nothing so much as a bantam cock strutting around looking for a fight, and the angry purr of his engine comes to me like the deep and continuous growl of a dog—if you will pardon the rapid exchange of metaphor.

"Save for this restless 'klik-klok!' and the booming of guns and the occasional whine of a shell as it passes over us, seeking for our howitzer batteries in the rear, the scene is peaceful enough, and you might not believe that we had a terrible battle here a little time ago, but for the fact that between our trench and the German's lie dozens of little dark heaps which once were German soldiers. How small a man is when he's dead."

Yet, despite this seeming calmness, the British were preparing for trouble. Mining operations were in progress. Underneath this trench which my friend so graphically described, and all unknown to the men who occupied it, stealthy work was going on. Far away in the rear, where the ground dropped down a little, men had dug an opening in the side of the slope. They had dug all day and all night, and gradually they had disappeared from view. The working party had first a dozen, and then another dozen had come, and then more men, with timber and with mine props, and they had disappeared into the black cavity to make firm the ground which had been dug out.

Then the diggers began to arrive in companies.

There was a great deal of earth to remove. As fast as the men at the head end of the tunnel cut through the soft earth, others shovelled it backward, yet others continued the passing until the earth they displaced reached the mouth of the tunnel and daylight. You may, if you give your imagination full rein, see plank roads laid in this earth gallery, and ceaseless trains of men with wheel-barrows filled with earth moving back to the mouth. You may picture all the subterfuge, all the secrecy and all the devices which were necessary to hide the work, so that no inkling of it should come to the watchful enemy.

Officers of the Royal Engineers planned and directed the work, organising the shifts and arranging by compass and instrument the direction the tunnel should take. What difficulties this mining party had we have not heard. We do not know of the unexpected things it encountered, of the detours it had to make to avoid this obstruction or the other. We only know that upon a certain day the Engineers found themselves under the side of Hill 60. Thereupon they began to construct transverse galleries, and to bring in the packages of dynamite or gun- cotton necessary for the great work in hand. And all the time sniping was going on overhead, the tiny attacks and counter- attacks, the night alarm, the bomb-throwings, and the thousand and one incidents which accompany modern warfare. Whilst men sweated in the depths of the earth their comrades in the air had not been idle. The British airman had established his ascendancy to a remarkable extent from the very beginning of the war. He had done this by sheer bravery—if one searched a book of synonyms from end to end one would not find a more appropriate word to describe the case than this word, bald as it is.

"Whenever we see a German aeroplane we attack it. If an airman sees two he attacks the two. We never expect a challenge, for the simple reason that the German has now come to such a pass that he never challenges. When we talk of ascendancy over the German, that is what we mean. The German is frightened of us in the air."

While the final touches were being put to the deadly little underground chambers beneath Hill 60, a striking proof of this ascendancy was seen. A British aeroplane engaged in reconnaissance espied a German rival in the distance. Oblivious to the peppering shells which were now coming up from the German anti-aircraft guns, the pilot at once turned his machine in the direction of his enemy. The German attempted to escape, but was headed off. He swept down to his own lines, but the British airman came after him, the observer shooting all the time at the petrol tank of his enemy. Then the German must have lost his nerve, for he started climbing again, and headed for the British lines, the British airman close in pursuit and climbing after him. The two armies stood still and watched this combat in the air. At last a shot from the British airman disabled the engine of the German, and he came gliding to earth behind the British lines. His foe alighted only a few feet from where the German had descended.

During this period, in two or three days, five aeroplanes were either driven down from the upper regions by British and French airmen, or were shot down by the soldiers in the trenches.
Whilst these local combats, of such dramatic interest to the men, who themselves lived in an atmosphere of drama, were being fought out, the greater business of the air service was being carried forward. Aeroplanes climbed up from the British lines to a height which precluded any danger from shell fire, and winged their way across country, making no attempt en route to disturb the equanimity of local forces. They were seeking for bigger game: for junctions packed with trains, for railway sidings filled with troops, for masses of infantry and artillery marching across country, and for those new formations as to the movements of which whispers had already reached the Headquarters Staff. They circled the Belgian border, they even penetrated to above German territory; they saw trains and camps, great motor convoys, batteries of guns, and came winging back to the British Headquarters with news that the enemy was indeed moving in strength against the thin line which Belgian and French and British were holding against the German advance on Calais. An official despatch told us that our airmen had on one day bombarded seven railway junctions with effect.

For the reader to understand all that the coming attack on Hill 60 signified, he must appreciate something of the objectives of modern warfare.

No longer does a wise General consider such things as geographical or political frontiers. That is to say, he is not greatly concerned, depressed, or elated by the fact that he is fighting in any particular geographical position, whether he be in his own country or in the territory of the enemy. The true frontiers in time of war are represented by the line which your enemy holds. Advantage is gained when that "frontier" is pierced, and when the terrain which is in his possession is in turn occupied by you. That is one point. The next point is almost as important: to obtain the initiative—that is to say, make your enemy's movements conform to yours—and at the same time produce, by that initiative, an offensive on his part which will bring him against your entrenched position.

Just as a clever boxer will allow his adversary to tire himself out in fruitless attacks, reserving his own strength to deal a knock-out blow, so does a modern General welcome any opportunity of provoking attack upon the part of his enemy. Especially does he welcome it when he has the advantage in numbers, in moral and in material.

It would seem that Field-Marshal Sir John French deliberately set out to engage the attention of all these extra bodies which were coming down into Flanders, and that he regarded the moment as propitious for the attraction of these large enemy forces. You may provoke attack on the part of your enemy by carrying his position at great sacrifice, by general assault. You lose a very large number of men in comparison with the number your enemy loses; but if you can gain your ground your object is half achieved, because he cannot leave you in undisputed possession and must return and deliver an offensive in as great force as you have employed to take the stronghold, and he must suffer losses corresponding to those which were endured by you when you delivered the attack which placed you in possession of the enemy's position.

The Field-Marshal had no desire to make great sacrifices. Propitious as the moment was, he could see no advantage which might be gained which would correspond to the losses he must endure. You may be sure that all the plans for the taking of Hill 60 were long since made, and the coming of the new formations fairly accurately timed.

Towards the end of the week which ended on April 17, the enemy before St. Éloi began to grow a little restive, and to give indication of a renewal of activity. News of the driving of a mine towards their main position had leaked through to the German lines; but exactly to where that mine passage was leading the enemy could have no accurate information.

Had his airman been able to serve him as well as the British airmen served our own army, he could have learnt perhaps of troops moving up in the neighbourhood of St. Éloi. At any rate, to meet our attack the Germans had busied themselves with preparing a few counter-mines, and these were exploded, not beneath the trenches confronting Hill 60, but farther south in the neighbourhood of Givenchy.

This was an ill-judged effort, greeted by our troops with ironical cheers, and no damage was done. On the morning of Saturday, the 17th, there were the customary exchanges, and a certain amount of local excitement was created by the destruction of one of the enemy's Minenwerfer, which was finished off by a howitzer battery. There was, too, yet another pretty fight in the air (the hero of which was Garros, the French airman), with tragic results to the German pilot, who was killed, and to the German observer who, by means of the dual control, brought the aeroplane safely to the British lines. That day our own airmen were exercising unusual vigilance. Otherwise, a bold observer, able to keep the British sentinels of the air at bay, would have seen the British trenches packed with men, as full as they could possibly hold, every reserve and support trench equally well occupied, and would have discovered, with the exercise of some prescience, evidence that something unusual was going forward.

The soldiers in the trenches themselves knew very little of what was coming. The officers went their rounds, seeing that each man was ready to attack, that the reserves of ammunition were to hand, and that the men were supplied with the rations they would require. There was an electric feeling in the air and knowledge that something unusual was going forward, and these men of ours, lying in the parapets, waited for the word "Go!"

The chill of evening had come. The east was already growing to a dull dun, when those who were looking toward Hill 60 saw an enormous fountain of earth and debris leap suddenly from its side, so that the hill was obscured in a fog of dust and smoke, saw a bright flicker as of lightning, and felt the earth shake and tremble beneath their feet in the terrifying roar of an explosion. Seven of the mines we had laid with such care had been fired simultaneously under the German trenches.

"Come on!" roared the commanding officer in one section of the trench, and the men, breaking from their cover, ran across the intervening space which separated them from the German trench, carried the first and the second line at the point of the bayonet, and ran up the hill, flinging themselves into the hot craters which the explosion had made.

"The interval that elapsed before our assault took place was—to use the words of one soldier—like a transformation scene. Trenches, parapets, sandbags disappeared, and the whole surface of the ground assumed strange shapes, here torn into huge craters, there forming mounds of fallen debris. "As the reports of the explosions died away, and while the dense columns of smoke and dust still hung in the air, our men, led by their officers, sprang from the trenches and rushed across the intervening space of some forty to sixty yards, lying between our line and the gaping craters before them, the front covered by the attack being only some 250 yards in length.

"Where the mines had actually exploded nothing was left of the occupants of the hostile line; but in the neighbouring trenches our assaulting infantry witnessed an extraordinary scene. Many of the German soldiers, possibly owing to the fact that they were working, were surprised in their shirt-sleeves without equipment.

"Stunned by the violence of the explosion, bewildered, and suddenly subjected to a rain of hand-grenades thrown by our bombing parties, they gave way to panic. Cursing and shouting, they were falling over one another and fighting in their hurry to gain the exits into the communication trenches; and some of those in rear, maddened by terror, were driving their bayonets into the bodies of their comrades in front."

First up the hill was "A" Company of the Queen's Own Royal West Kent Regiment, with "B" in support, and "C" and "D" in reserve. Then came the companies of the King's Own Scottish Borderers, the West Riding Regiment, the Yorkshire Light Infantry, and the Victoria Rifles (City of London T.F.). It was the indomitable 13th Brigade—that brigade which had hammered its way down from Mons to the Marne, which had stood the hard knocks of battle and the bitter trials of winter, and now came as fresh as ever to the work of assault.

The enemy were momentarily paralysed. At first, even in the trenches which stretched left and right, though they fought desperately, the steel had gone out of their resistance.

But the Germans quickly recovered from their surprise, and it was then that the real struggle began. From our line the hill was exposed to fire from three sides, and it was only a few moments before the German gunners took advantage of this fact and opened fire. Soon the whole position became obscured in the smoke of bursting shells.

(I am drawing from the vivid description supplied by "Eye-Witness.")

"Meanwhile, our batteries had begun to support the attack, and a terrific artillery fire was maintained far into the night.

"As darkness fell the scene was grand in the extreme. From many points along our line to the north and south of Hill 60 could be seen the flashes of the shells, while those of the guns were so nearly continuous as to resemble the effect of musketry. Under this fire our men had to work, throwing up parapets towards the enemy, blocking their communications, and generally rendering the position defensible.

"Nor were the enemy's infantry idle. Advancing up the communication trenches, they threw hand-grenades over the barricades and also into the mine crater, on the crumbling sides of which our men were clinging in the endeavour to obtain a foothold."

The British infantry gained the crest, and far into the darkness of the night they worked with entrenching tools, spades, and wire, to put themselves into a state of defence.

The first counter-attack came in the night. It was half-hearted and was hammered back mercilessly. The second shared no better fate, the hillside was left piled with dead. The tireless infantry worked like galley slaves, filling their sandbags, creating their new parapets and communicating trenches, and at dawn Hill 60 was better defended than it had ever been defended before—only this time the parapets faced the German front.

The Germans came back half-heartedly at first. It may have needed the application of those cat-o'-nine-tails which the British discovered in the German trenches before Neuve Chapelle to get these men, shocked and shaken by their terrific experience of the evening, to return in a vain effort to drive the British forth.

At seven in the morning the serious counter-assault was delivered. All night long the trains had been disgorging troops at Roulers. Frantic telegrams had been bringing the scattered corps to this front; and now at seven o'clock arrayed against the devoted brigade which held the crest of Hill 60, came the flower of the German Army. Prussian and Bavarian swept up the hill in solid mass. Waiting in the rear of the British lines to see at what point the attempt would be directed were our side-car machine-guns. When no doubt existed any longer as to the front which would bear the brunt of the assault, these nimble engines of war came tearing to their appointed stations. Into the German mass the machine-guns poured their ceaseless stream of lead, and the attacking line melted and dwindled away. Again the British came out with the bayonet, and again they swept victoriously down the slope of the hill, driving before them the remnants of a very gallant force.

All night long, as the infantry had worked, the enemy had flung shell after shell over their position, and the firing was intensified throughout the day, and under its support yet another attack was made on the Sunday evening, which gave the Germans a foothold in our trenches on the southern edge of the hill.

They were not to enjoy their possession for long. Help reached our front line in the form of reinforcements who swept the Germans from the foothold they had gained, and our position became more secure. British wounded had been left behind in those trenches which the German occupied, and British wounded at Neuve Chapelle had been battered and hacked to death by these ruthless butchers. Back came the British with the bayonet, even as they had come at Neuve Chapelle, when young Madden had fallen dying with the cry: "Come on, the King's!" on his lips. Back they went in irresistible floods, pouring into the trench that the German had won with such labour, and driving such of its occupants as were left alive down the slope of the hill. Little they cared, these British soldiers, though battery after battery of German artillery came into action, VOL. III. D and the hill side was ablaze with the light of bursting shells. It was now that our casualties came heavily. In the dark of the night the grey infantry came up again to dispute possession of the hill, and again in hand-to-hand fighting they were driven back, leaving behind a further sprinkling of dead. Left and right along the line, almost to the region of Neuve Chapelle, as far as Bixschoote, the sector was alight, and the ceaseless rattle of rifle fire and the constant booming and crashing of heavy guns ran beyond earshot on either flank.

The fight for Neuve Chapelle, St. Éloi and Hill 60 took a very heavy toll of British lives, but it must be remembered that the fighting was on a much larger scale than it had ever been since the British Army has been in France. Of the troops employed we have only heard of the 4th Corps, and especially of the 7th Division, whose gallant defence of Ypres was one of the outstanding features of the war. The 1st Army was generally engaged, and it was to Sir Douglas Haig that Sir John French paid his greatest tribute. Some British regiments lost almost all their officers. The Cameronians lost, in one day's fighting, fifteen officers killed and nine wounded. This was, I suppose, at St. Éloi, and possibly the Cameronians suffered the full force of the enemy's first attack. The Devonshire Regiment, the Highland Light Infantry, and the Argyll and Sutherland Highlanders, the Black Watch, the Cameron Highlanders, the Royal Scots, and the Gordon Highlanders were in the thick of it. To the list of Scottish Regiments must be added the heavy casualties of the Seaforth Highlanders, who lost fifteen officers killed and wounded. The casualty list of this regiment in the neighbourhood of Neuve Chapelle and La Bassée had been a very heavy one. The Seaforths, it will be remembered, held the orchard to the north of Festubert against a series of determined attacks, held fast until the arrival of reinforcements to relieve them. The steadfastness of the Seaforths was a characteristic feature throughout the whole campaign. I have previously referred to that excellent unit, the Middlesex Regiment, and if I again refer to the splendid corps which were fighting Britain's battles, and enlarge upon the traditions and the individual character of these regiments it is because, behind the cold and formal account which was published from official sources, there lies the individual heroism, which is so dear to the British heart.

Where the Argylls were we may be sure the Middlesex would be. But the Middlesex must have found a particularly hot corner, as their losses showed. Of the Irish regiments, the Irish Rifles were engaged, the Inniskilling Fusiliers, the Dublin Fusiliers, and the Leinsters.

Yet other mentioned regiments were the Lincolns, the Northamptonshire Regiment, the Sherwood Foresters, and the Worcestershire Regiment, which had the largest casualty roll of all.

It has been an extraordinary feature of this war that the names of certain regiments have recurred again and again. I have already touched upon this in describing the fighting about Givenchy, and the list of casualties in the operations at Neuve Chapelle and St. Éloi merely emphasises the point. Again and again had the Worcesters appeared as being in the van of some desperate enterprise. The Northamptonshire Regiment had an unbroken record of fine achievements, starting at the very beginning of the war and continuing almost without a break from month to month. In almost every despatch which General French has sent us he spoke of this fine regiment. It is remembered as the corps which delivered an attack through the mists on the Aisne and carried a line of trenches, driving the Germans up the hill. Then there are the Sherwood Foresters and the Lincolns, whose names are constantly cropping up in official despatches. These heavy casualties in certain regiments show one thing, namely, that the traditions which have been gained in this war were bearing immediate fruit. The proud name which certain regiments have made for themselves were being upheld worthily by their successors, and men preferred to stand and die at their posts, so long as they could accomplish the purpose which they were put to accomplish, rather than retire, even in the face of an overwhelming attack.

The Indian troops, said Sir John French in a message to the Viceroy of India, fought with great gallantry and marked success in the capture of Neuve Chapelle and the subsequent fighting. The fighting was very severe and their losses heavy, but nothing daunted them. Their tenacity, courage, and endurance were admirable.

CHAPTER V — THE SECOND ATTACK ON YPRES

Thursday, April 22, was such a day as compensated for the long and dreary winter, for the blizzards and the rain, and the bleak unlovely outlook which had been the soldiers' throughout the dark winter months of the war. An almost cloudless sky, a gentle northerly breeze, and a flood of yellow sunlight made even the trenches tolerable habitations, and gave to the gossiping soldiers who crowded them north and south of Ypres a sense of well-being.

Along the line, on either side of the Ypres salient, the men in the trenches had heard the ceaseless thunder of guns about Hill 60, had seen the midnight skies aglow with bursting shells, and had wondered who in the argot of the trenches was "getting it."

"We heard and practically saw the fighting, and we said: 'They are having another cut at Ypres,'" wrote a soldier to his mother from Neuve Chapelle. "They'll be down after us shortly, but we are ready for them."

But the German was not moving southward.

The alert British airmen, who were constantly above the German lines, detected certain concentrations of troops, movements of artillery, and the transport of heavy wagons; but these were going northward, toward that section of line which was held by a colonial division of the French Army.

Ypres was defended by a succession of trenches to the east of the town, by a semi-circular formation which passed to the west of Gheluvelt, straddled the Ypres-Roulers railway, and continued between the village of St. Julien and Poelcapelle to a tributary of the Yser (the Yserlée), and so south of Dixmude to the edge of the flooded area. The British line itself ran up from Givenchy through Armentières to Neuve Chapelle, St. Éloi, and then to the east of Ypres, where, as already stated, a French division formed a link between the Belgian and British forces.

The extreme left of the British line was held on April 22 by two brigades of the Canadian division, the first brigade being in general reserve. Nearer to Ypres were the British regular and Territorial battalions, and the nearer they were to Hill 60, the more actively were they engaged with the enemy upon their front.

The German had failed entirely to recover the ground he had lost at Hill 60, and indeed until the crest of Hill 60 was all but swept away by fire, we held on to that position. He had failed in spite of the fact that he had employed large masses, that he had been wasteful of life, and had flung his men, with a certain prodigal disregard for consequences, at the unshaken line that now circled the hill. He might hope, with some reason, to force this position, and not only this position, but the Ypres salient, by delivering an attack upon a portion of the line to the north or to the south which was not strongly held. Southward, any attempt was foredoomed to failure. St. Éloi and Givenchy, no less than Neuve Chapelle, had taught him the futility of attempting to carry those positions unless he had available a force much larger than he possessed.

He seemed to have set to work with extraordinary thoroughness to procure the retirement of the connecting French link, and through the gap thus formed (some 4,200 yards) to push in every available man he could muster, not with the object of reaching the coast, as some people imagined, but in order to thrust so tight a wedge into the Allied lines as, for preservation's sake, would compel his enemy to bring about either the immediate retirement of the Belgian army, which was holding the Yser, or else the flattening out of the Ypres salient.

Some time during April 19 the German had distributed along his front trenches, confronting the French, a number of cylinders, probably similar in appearance to those in which hydrogen and oxygen are "packed" in this country, and these were filled at great pressure with a gas which had terrible asphyxiating effects upon its victims.

It was a gas which, because of its specific gravity, remains close to the ground and is not easily dispersed. It was originally intended by the German, as we ascertained later from a deserter, to employ this barbarous weapon on the 20th, but the winds were unfavourable.

The French trenches ran due east and west, and it was necessary, for the success of the German plan, that there should be a fresh northerly wind blowing, which would carry the vapours, when they were released, into the French lines.

The opportunity came on the Thursday, and at five o'clock in the afternoon the gases were simultaneously released all along the German front, and floated in a thick yellow vapour. The puzzled French watched this slow-moving curtain of mist coming toward them, and thought at first it was merely a ruse to veil the approach of German troops.

With this idea in their minds they opened a vigorous fusillade upon the German trenches—a fusillade somewhat disconcerting to the enemy, who had already risen over their parapets and were waiting for the asphyxiating gas to do its work before they rushed forward and occupied their enemy's line.

The first conviction of danger came to the French when the mist came pouring into their trenches, seeking the lower levels. Instantly the officers realised the dastardly trick which was being played upon them, and realised, too, the impossibility of holding out under these conditions.

The Turcos who comprised the French force scrambled out of their trenches and began to make for the second line. Many fell, gasping in agony, struggling for their breath; others were shot down; only a very few managed to reach the supporting trenches before the inexorable vapour came rolling across over the ground, flooding the second trench line in exactly the same way and driving its occupants to retreat.

The Canadians, to the right of the French and on the extreme left of the British line, watched this withdrawal, to them inexplicable, in amazement. They noticed the yellow veil of mist which moved with the wind, but saw little in this to excite their apprehension.

Their own line was secure. Behind them, in a patch of wood, were their four heavy guns, which that morning had been shelling the enemy line, and the presence of big guns in the vicinity of infantry has invariably a tendency to generate confidence. At any rate, they themselves had no reason to expect any immediate attack or any unusual pressure to be placed upon their front.

It was a Canadian officer on the extreme left, watching through his glasses the progress of this curious "smoke," who soon awoke to the fact that the French had retired and that there existed a gap in the line of more than a mile in length. Instantly the news was flashed to Brigadier-General Turner, commanding the 3rd Brigade, and he was the first to grasp the nature of the disaster which was imminent.

His flank was left uncovered to a very strong German force, The guns in the rear, they were immediately in the rear of the junction between French and Canadians, were jeopardised, even though they were two miles away. With commendable promptitude he extended his line to the left, intending to bend it back so that it would rest upon the wood. Necessarily, with this manoeuvre many of the Canadians came under the influence of the noxious gases which were still distributed over the ground. Men went suddenly blue in the face, staggered and fell. Others came reeling forth, choking and gasping, for the gas immediately attacked the lung passage and the bronchial tubes, and set up, in a remarkably short space of time, a condition which may be described as acute bronchitis. Quick as the Canadian commander had been, the enemy had been quicker to take advantage of the inevitable confusion caused by his foul warfare and by the necessity hurriedly to readjust the Canadian position. Sweeping forward, supported by huge bodies of men, all protected against the fumes of the gas area which they had to penetrate by pads fastened over their noses and mouths, the Germans reached the wood where the guns were long before the first extension of the line came in touch. It was hopeless for the first little party which came under fire from the wood to make any attempt at saving the guns. They had to face heavy fusillades and attacks along their front, extending even as far as the right of the 2nd Brigade. Later that 2nd Brigade, whose line was intact, had to fall back slowly upon the village of St. Julien, but in the first hours of attack it held steadily to its position. The German rush was overwhelming, and the guns passed into the enemy's possession. The country was flat, broken only by those thick hedges which the Belgian farmer erects at every hundred metres. Save for the wood, the plain was innocent of trees, and even those which formed the copse where the guns were concealed were thin, almost reed-like saplings of no great height. Cover there was none save that which the men made for themselves. But behind these lines trenches had already been prepared, and into these the Canadians crowded.

In the meantime the news of the calamity, for such it undoubtedly was, had gone back to Divisional and to Corps Headquarters.

Some of the retiring Turcos had straggled to the confines of Ypres itself, and formed the centre of a dozen inquiring knots of British soldiers who wanted to know what all the trouble was about. For this kind of retirement, unaccompanied by any very heavy preparatory fire, was inexplicable. The artillery bombardment, which as a rule precedes a violent assault, in this case followed it, and even as the soldiers were interrogating the bewildered Turcos, a terrific bombardment was opened upon Ypres.

They had not long to wait, these hardened soldiers of Great Britain, before they learnt the seriousness of the attack and the manner in which it affected them personally. A staff officer rode his sweating horse at a gallop through the lines and shouted a sharp order. "Nothing more impressive can be imagined," wrote "Eye-Witness", "than the sight of our men falling in quickly in perfect order on their alarm posts amid the scene of wild confusion caused by the panic-stricken refugees who swarmed along the roads."

In ten minutes the British regiments were moving across the plain slope towards the scene of the fighting.

But the Canadians were not waiting for assistance. Bitterly chagrined at the position in which they found themselves, humiliated by the loss of their guns, they needed no incentive to make an attempt at their recovery. They were fresh from England, with the memory still green of wet and tiresome days on Salisbury Plain, of their anguish of mind when, morning after morning, no fresh instructions had reached them to move to the front. And then one day that electric order had arrived, and they had gone out to Flanders full of hope, full of determination, and full of enthusiasm. They had passed under the approving eye of their commander-in-chief; they had borne the exacting and critical scrutiny of the war-worn soldiers of Britain; and they had gone into the trenches to await the supreme test with the words of their General ringing in their ears: "It is the boast of my old regiment that they never budge from a trench. I want you to be able to say the same when the war ends."

A few of them had been driven back by fumes. The remainder had had to alter their line because of the French retirement. But the fact that their guns were in the hands of the enemy rankled more with the Canadians than it would with a regular regiment. For the regular would have accepted the position with a philosophy and a humour which would in no way have weakened his effort to recover the lost cannon.

The Canadians were sensitive, wrathful, burning with a desire to undo the mischief which the German had caused by his employment of methods to which civilisation had denied its approval. The sun went down on the hurried movement of the Canadians, who, company by company, and regiment by regiment, were gradually shifting to a new front, moving in seeming confusion toward their left, so that the new Canadian line resembled a triangle with its apex immediately south of Poelcapelle. It went down, too, upon the sturdy khaki columns coming up from Ypres, moving with strides which would have appeared to the tyro to be leisurely, until he realised that it is the object of a commanding officer to get troops into the fighting line with as little fatigue as possible, and to present them at the trench, where their supreme effort had to be made, in such condition as would enable them to put forth their best work.

"The British are coming up in support," was the word that ran down the line.

The 1st Canadian Brigade, which had been in general reserve, was already moving up. A misty moon showed the dark masses of Canadians forming for an attack upon the left. They had not been allowed to continue or conclude their preparations for this attack in peace.

The whole weight of German metal had been thrown against the new Canadian salient, and the Canadian Division was terribly outnumbered. Fire flamed at them from forty thousand rifles; massed machine-guns sprayed their front with nickel; guns of every calibre pounded these men who formed up as if on parade, knowing that they were going to annihilation, yet joyful at the prospect.

The Canadian Scottish (the 16th Battalion of the 3rd Brigade) and the 10th Battalion of the 2nd Brigade had been intercepted on their way to reserve trenches, and had been sent to this front. These two battalions, commanded by Lieutenant-Colonel Leckie and Lieutenant-Colonel Boyle, were given the task of clearing the small wood and recovering the guns. But the enemy had utilised his time well. He had entrenched himself at the edge of the wood; he had hurried forward his light Maxims and had literally banked them on the front where an attack was to be expected.

"We never thought there was a chance of your taking the wood," said a German prisoner afterwards. "I heard my colonel say: 'It is too much to hope that they will come up against us here.' We knew you were Canadians and we thought you might try, but we were so certain that any attack would be utterly defeated that some of our men lay down and went to sleep."

They were awakened soon enough. A waving line of bayonets flickered in the pale moonlight as the Canadians came in a jog-trot, halting only to pour volley after volley into the little wood, while the British guns, concentrating their fire, dropped shell after shell into the enemy's cover. Then with a roar of cheering, the Canadians were up, over the first barricade and into the enemy's trenches, hacking and stabbing with their bayonets. In that wood, where the trees grew so thickly that men had to pick their way to get through, the Canadians poured, driving the enemy in retreat.

The official Observer with the Canadian Division gave us a vivid idea of this stage of the struggle. "An officer who took part in the attack describes how the men about him fell under the fire of the machine-guns, which, in his phrase, played upon them 'like a watering-pot.' He added, quite simply, 'I wrote my own life off.' But the line never wavered.

"When one man fell another took his place, and with a final shout the survivors of the two battalions flung themselves into the wood. The German garrison was completely demoralised, and the impetuous advance of the Canadians did not cease until they reached the far side of the wood and entrenched themselves there in the position so dearly gained. They had, however, the disappointment of finding that the guns had been blown up by the enemy."

The Canadians pushed through to the farther edge of the wood and held on to a trench line, and gradually the gaps on their right and between themselves and the main body were filled up as the new Canadian regiments came into action. Throughout the earlier part of the night the position, which was gained at such cost, was held by the gallant Canadians.

"The fighting continued all through the night, and to those who observed the indications that the attack was being pushed with ever-growing strength, it hardly seemed possible that the Canadians, fighting in positions so difficult to defend, could maintain their resistance for any long period."

Then, in the early hours of the morning, the enemy brought a concentrated fire to bear upon the wood. It was such a fire as the most seasoned soldier had seldom seen.

"It swept the wood as a tropical storm sweeps the leaves of the forest," said the official Observer, "and it made it impossible for them to hold the position for which they had sacrificed so much." The little plantation became a chaos of shattered and burning tree trunks, flying branches were hurled in all directions, and it was in this period probably that the Canadian engaged on this front suffered his severest losses. If he had not rescued the guns, he had at least the satisfaction of knowing that he had forced the enemy to make them useless, and under the heavy fire which was opened on him he had no other course to pursue than to retire. This he did in good order, taking his wounded with him.

So far from the enemy's attack weakening, it gained in intensity as the night wore through, and in the early hours of the morning the confused line which the Canadian had hastily constructed toward St. Julien was assailed with such ferocity as to render it doubtful in the minds of the Staff whether it was possible to hold on any longer.

And here let us consider the Canadian, whose baptism of fire had been so frightful. He was untrained to war, he was, to all intents and purposes, indeed by the duration of his service, a raw recruit. Yet his demeanour and attitude in that moment of terrible ordeal were that of a seasoned warrior. Calm, confident, alert, taking no thought for his own life and determined at all hazards to be worthy of the uniform he wore, he displayed a resolution and a courage which were wholly disconcerting to his enemy.

"The English brought their old Army up in the night," said a German officer prisoner, describing what had happened; but in truth he was mistaken. The "Old Army," which withstood the weight of the heavy German attack delivered on one small front of an army corps, was a brigade and a half of Canadians.

With the coming of daylight, the seriousness of the whole British position became apparent. It was not now a question of guns, their loss or their recovery; it was not a question, even, of retaining this or that line of trenches; it was a matter of holding the British line intact and preventing the German from thrusting a wedge between the Belgian and the British—a wedge which would broaden as it progressed, and must in the course of a few days, as new German troops were rushed to the spot, have the effect of isolating and completely surrounding the Belgian Army and its gallant King.

It is a moot point, and one which I have already discussed in a previous chapter, as to whether the German had sufficient armed men to enable him to carry out such a project; but it is not difficult to understand that, once he had succeeded in driving a wedge into the line, he could afford to weaken other points, even taking the troops he had reserved for possible employment against Italy, in order to procure so immeasurable an advantage which a success upon the West would have given him. The daylight showed the British commander new and denser masses upon his left, and he could be in no doubt that the German intended to secure his envelopment at whatever cost. Gradually the grey lines were flowing round the jagged ends of the Canadian line. The gap which had been left by the retirement of the Turcos had not by any means been filled. Farther back, on his new front, the middle line was patchily held. The British troops which had been brought up to strengthen the line had so far directed their efforts toward the salvation of the position near St. Julien. Whatever had to be done in the way of checking the threatened development, had to be done quickly, and it had to be done, moreover, by the Canadians themselves.

They might wait and see what the German intention was and place themselves in a position of defence in order to counteract the enemy plans; but such a course of action would have been attended by the greatest risks. The Canadian general saw his duty, and saw it plainly. It was to make a counter-attack upon this growing horde, and endeavour to force them from the trench lines which they now occupied and which would serve to cover further encroachments by the invader. That first line of German trenches, it must be remembered, was well in behind the trenches previously occupied by the French—so far had the enemy advanced.

The Canadian commander's decision was not lightly taken, for he had no illusions as to the strength of the German position or his ability to defend himself. The men in the trenches were undoubtedly troops of vast war experience, and it was asking something of new troops, who were having their first experience of war, to deliver a frontal attack in such circumstances. Whatever hesitation the Canadian general had did not last very long. As for the men, they were anxious and impatient for the trial of strength. A British brigade had now come upon the scene, and this, with the Ontario 1st and 4th Battalions of the 1st Brigade, under Brigadier-General Mercer, moved forth to the task which awaited them.

As they came across the plain a veritable cascade of fire fell upon these devoted ranks. Men fell left and right, but others came up into their places. Slowly at first, then gaining speed as they neared their objective, Briton and Canadian pressed on side by side.

"It is safe to say," wrote the Canadian Observer in his despatch, "that the youngest private in the ranks, as he set his teeth for the advance, knew the task in front of him, and the youngest subaltern knew all that rested upon his success. It did not seem that any human being could live in the shower of shot and shell which began to play upon the advancing troops.

"They suffered terrible casualties. For a short time every other man seemed to fall, but the attack was pressed ever closer and closer. The 4th Canadian Battalion at one moment came under a particularly withering fire. For a moment— not more—it wavered. Its most gallant commanding officer, Lieut.-Colonel Burchill, carrying, after an old fashion, a light cane, coolly and cheerfully rallied his men, and at the very moment when his example had infected them fell dead at the head of his battalion.

"With a hoarse cry of anger they sprang forward (for, indeed, they loved him) as if to avenge his death. The astonishing attack which followed, pushed home in the face of direct frontal fire, made in broad daylight, by battalions whose names should live for ever in the memories of soldiers, was carried to the first line of German trenches. After a hand-to-hand struggle, the last German who resisted was bayoneted, and the trench was won."

"We were in the trenches before we knew where we were," said a man who took part in that wonderful charge; "and the Germans had to decide whether they wanted to live or die, and had to decide quick. Every man who did not instantly put up his arms was bayoneted, and we left the trench filled with German dead."

If you place the letter S upon its side thus, the first curve will represent the points where this charge was made, the other curve the salient of Ypres, and it will be easy to see the enormous consequence which attended the Canadian success in this sector.

They were attacking the most advanced point of the German wedge which had been driven into the Allied line, and not only did they so attack, in face of a withering fire, but they clinched their victory in their hand-to-hand fight, in which prodigies of valour were performed. A huge Canadian sergeant cleared one communication trench single-handed, parried a bomb, which was thrown at him, with the point of his bayonet, and killed the officer who was directing a German section with one blow from the butt of his rifle. A Canadian private, wounded to death, shouted as his comrades passed: "Kill a German for me. I'm done." And thus many men who fell urged their comrades forward as they died.

"The measure of this success may be taken when it is pointed out that this trench represented in the German advance the apex in the breach which the enemy had made in the original line of the Allies, and that it was two and a half miles south of that line. This charge, made by men who looked death indifferently in the face—for no man who took part in it could think that he was likely to live—saved, and that was much, the Canadian left.

"But it did more. Up to the point where the assailants conquered or died, it secured and maintained during the most critical moment of all the integrity of the Allied line."

Throughout Friday, Saturday, and Sunday these two regiments, hammered by the full weight of German artillery, held their own against every counter-attack which was delivered, clung to their trenches though a veritable inferno of artillery fire was opened upon them, though bomb and hand grenade, shell and shrapnel and machine-gun, were turned upon their front. But they held fast, in spite of all, until the night of Sunday, the 25th.

The two Canadian regiments engaged in the attack had not been involved in the first catastrophe. Being of the 1st Brigade, they had been in reserve somewhere in the rear, and had been hastily beaten up to close the gap between the Belgians and the British. In the meantime, the 3rd Brigade, which, as already stated, was at the extreme left of the line, were fully occupied in endeavouring to establish a communicating line between these two battalions of the 1st Brigade and the British. Though the bigger gap was closed, there was a wide interval on the left of the 3rd Brigade, which needed filling.

The position as it existed on the Friday morning, after the reserves had taken the "Wood of the Guns" and had retired, may be summed up by saying that each unit was confronted with the urgent necessity of battling for its own preservation, and was at the same time expected to render assistance to other units equally embarrassed. It was as though they were ordered to "Do your utmost and a little more."

Certainly, the 3rd Brigade, which so far had been the only body of the Canadians to feel the effect of the fumes, though in a less degree to that which the French had experienced, were hard pressed to hold their own. From five o'clock on Thursday evening throughout the night they had been subjected to a punishing fire. They could with ease have held the position they occupied on Thursday morning but for the necessity of weakening their ranks to extend their line to the south-west.

It was abundantly clear that the enemy's full strength was directed along a front of not more than 4,000 yards. He had crossed the Yser—but that was no fault of the Canadians.

The Belgians on the other side of the gap were pushing troops to the right, but our gallant little Ally had not sufficient men to spare. Moreover, the fury of German endeavour was directed against them also, and from behind the ruined walls and barricades of the little village of Lizerne they were contesting a terrific attack which had been launched simultaneously with that which had driven the French line in.

I have said that the first emission of gas by the Germans had scarcely affected the Canadian line, save those upon the extreme left of the 3rd Brigade, who had come in for the fringe of the mist. That discharge, however, had been intended solely for the benefit of the Turcos, and it was not until four o'clock on the Friday morning that the Germans brought their gas apparatus into play on the Canadian front. The poor fellows of the Canadian regiments who found themselves unable to escape these fumes, were instantly suffocated. The Highland Regiments of Canada, the Royal Highlanders of Montreal, the 48th Highlanders and two other battalions of Canadian infantry, the 13th and 15th, were specially affected by this new early morning attempt. The darkness before the dawn had hidden the approach of this slow-moving mist, and it was in the Canadian trenches before the men realised their terrible danger. The Royal Highlanders stood, vainly endeavouring to disperse the asphyxiating fumes, and the 48th Highlanders, who seem to have received a more than ordinary poisonous fog, were driven from their trenches, which were rendered intolerable. They did not go very far back, however, nor did they remain away for any length of time. Long before the Germans could reach the abandoned trench the Highlanders were back again, choking and coughing, but ready to punish the men who had descended to this method of warfare.

"It was terrible to see grown men tearing at their tunics, their shirts, to expose their bare breasts to the cold air of morning, gasping, livid and blue, fighting desperately for their breath, yet with their vengeful eyes peering across the parapet—mindful, in spite of their own terrible distress, of the business they had in hand."

The German attack at this point was a feeble one, and it was probably employed to mask the more important operations on their right. The enemy knew of the gap which existed between the 3rd Brigade and the newly formed line farther to the south, and the grey hordes were moving quickly to seize the advantage which that gap presented. For a short time the position of the 3rd Brigade was a parlous one, for several German divisions were attempting to overwhelm it. The enemy had slipped behind in the early hours of the morning, and direct communication with the brigade headquarters was cut off. Only the devotion of the left, which continued a succession of harassing attacks upon the enemy, saved the brigade from complete envelopment.

In that confused fighting, where men found their front continuously changed, and where companies and battalions raced across the open under heavy fire, to an unknown destination and to the attack of a force of unknown strength, the Canadians' mettle was tested tremendously. On the Royal Highlanders of Montreal and the 13th Battalion fell the heaviest of the fighting. Captain McCuaig, who had received very severe wounds, resolutely refused to be moved from his trench to safety, urging on his men to the greater business of smashing the German offensive. Major Norsworth, of the 13th Regiment, rallying his men cheerfully, although almost disabled by a bullet wound, was soon afterwards shot and bayoneted under the eyes of his company, who fought desperately about his body, and by the very fierceness of their attack drove back an enemy of vastly superior numbers. It was a case of hand-to-hand fighting, a case of holding on by nail and tooth, and though every moment showed the position to be more and more desperate and revealed to the Brigade commander increasing masses of Germans upon his left, the Canadians, obliged to retire, contested every step of the way. Captain McCuaig met his end as gloriously as Major Norsworth. Thus the Canadian Record Officer told the story of his heroic sacrifice.

"This most gallant officer was seriously wounded in a hurriedly-constructed trench at a moment when it would have been possible to remove him to safety. He absolutely refused to move, and continued in the discharge of his duty. But the situation grew constantly worse, and peremptory orders were received for an immediate withdrawal.

"Those who were compelled to obey them were most insistent to carry with them, at whatever risk to their own mobility and safety, an officer to whom they were devotedly attached. But he, knowing, it may be, better than they the exertions which still lay in front of them, and unwilling to inflict upon them the disabilities of a maimed man, very resolutely refused, and asked of them one thing only, that there should be given to him as he lay alone in the trench two loaded Colt revolvers to add to his own, which lay in his right hand as he made his last request. And so, with three revolvers ready to his hand for use, a very brave officer waited to sell his life, wounded and racked with pain, in an abandoned trench."

Such instances could be multiplied without effort. The Canadian men were splendid, their officers were magnificent. They were true to the traditions not only of their race but of their caste, and especially was this true of the Canadian Scots, who in the face of difficulties and dangers of extraordinary and unprecedented kinds, gave their lives cheerfully and sold them dearly for the Motherland.

And now the 3rd Brigade were moving back, leaving the detachment of Royal Highlanders and the 13th Regiment and the Royal Montreal Regiment and the 14th Battalion to make their way back as well as they could. It was impossible in that moment to bring about the retirement of every single man in a uniform line without jeopardising the safety of a whole brigade.

The apex of the position was now upon St. Julien, and the farther south the retirement was carried the stronger became the connecting line and the more obvious did it become to the German commander that he could not possibly hope to achieve the object which he had set out to secure. The chagrin of the enemy manifested itself in a renewed vigour of attack, in an almost senseless waste of ammunition.

The German objective had been twofold.

It had been, as a primary object, to force a wedge into the Allied line and to isolate the Belgian; it had also had probably as a secondary object, though most writers suggest it as the primary reason, the flattening out of the Ypres salient.

Yet Ypres, though its line was pinched so that it now struck sharply, like an acute angle, into the enemy's position, was untouched and unshaken, and the British, who had been battling desperately to retake their hold of Hill 60, and were now enjoying something of a lull, were as strongly entrenched about that famous mound as they could well be. With the retirement of the 3rd Brigade the brunt of the frontal attack must necessarily be borne by the 2nd, which had been only slightly affected up till now. The same condition as existed when the French moved back, exposing the 3rd Brigade, was reproduced to some extent by the enforced retreat of the 3rd. The Brigadier of the 2nd Brigade, which had maintained its lines, had had ample warning of his colleague's intention.

The village of St. Julien, which on Thursday morning had been well to the rear of the British line, and had probably furnished billets for a portion of the British force, was now the actual front, and it was hoped that the Canadians, aided by the British brigade which had come up and which had helped to form a "bottom" to the basin-shaped line which the German had created, would be able to arrest the enemy advance sufficiently to allow yet more troops to be brought up, and a portion of the lost ground regained.

The 2nd Brigade had held a front of about a mile and a half, and Brigadier-General Curry proceeded at once to drop back his left flank to cover St. Julien, which, however, was soon rendered untenable by enemy artillery and the line forced back to the south of that village.

It must be remembered that the 2nd Brigade were in touch with the British, holding the vital point which protected Ypres; and, splendid as had been the achievement of the Canadians on the left in picturesque and thrilling fighting, the burden of defence, so far as the east of the Ypres line was concerned, necessarily fell upon Brigadier-General Curry's brigade.

Obviously, if the 2nd had shared the fate of the 3rd, and if they in turn had been driven back uniformly, and the attack against their trench lines had succeeded, a general retirement before Ypres, and possibly the evacuation of that town, would have been rendered imperative.

From Thursday at five o'clock until Sunday afternoon the 2nd Brigade held its newly organised line. And on Sunday afternoon they had not abandoned their trenches. "There were none left. They had been obliterated by artillery fire." The extreme left of the 2nd Brigade was held by the 90th Winnipeg Rifles.

For the first time the German was meeting a new force.

He had met the French Canadians of Montreal; he had crumbled before the impetuous charge of the American Canadians of Toronto, and now he was to meet the men of the Western plains—those fearless soldiers from the prairies of Manitoba.

Winnipeg had sent this battalion forth in pride and confidence, to represent the great corn lands of the West in the struggle which the Motherland was waging against the tyrant of Europe; and well was that confidence repaid.

The line, newly adjusted, held against the hammer blows which were delivered by the trained soldiers of the Kaiser. Again and again, with a reckless disregard for life, were the German battalions flung at this unshaken front, but ever it held.

Then the German tried his gas upon the 90th, loosened the caps of his cylinders close at hand, and sent the men from Winnipeg fighting for air, dazed, blinded and choking, back to their support trenches. In triumph the German, occupied the trenches which the Canadians had abandoned, but their stay was a short one. Well might they doubt the efficacy of their last brutal method when, very silently, the 90th crept back with the bayonet, destroyed the occupants of their trenches, flung out the dead and established themselves again on the line from which they had been ejected.
The 90th held on even when the 3rd Brigade had gone back and when the gap between them and their nearest troops became greater and greater. The enemy could not have known that this heaven-sent opportunity had been presented to him, until it was too late to take advantage of it. Then he hurried forward his reserves to cut in behind the 90th, but they arrived too late. Two British regiments came up on Saturday night, filled the "hole" which the retirement had occasioned; and the German, who marched forward, as he thought, to an unresisting front, was met by that methodical fire, slow and sure and unhurried, which told him that he was in the presence of the "old" Army.

The left of the 2nd Brigade was now south of St. Julien, "fighting every yard." That village had been taken in the morning, and had seemingly left a clear way of advance—a way of which the enemy did not immediately avail himself. Fire was intensified; the attacks came heavier and heavier instead of diminishing; but the Canadian troops, who had not slept, many of them, for 72 hours, displayed a fortitude in defence which must arouse the wonder of all those who have not seen the soldier in action and the admiration of the military world.

The part the old Army had taken in this fight (by "old Army" I mean, of course, the regular regiments of the British Army which have served throughout the war) has already been described. They, with two Canadian regiments, formed the bottom of the basin, whilst two British battalions had come up to extend the left of the 2nd Brigade and keep touch with the retiring 3rd. We had at this time a very large army in Flanders and France numbering hundreds of thousands, and so far not more than 30,000 British, probably considerably less, had been engaged in the actual firing line at this portion of the field.

It might seem a simple matter to bring troops from reserve, especially when it was obvious that a permanent breach of the line would be attended by disastrous consequences; but the Commander-in-Chief of the British Army must keep his eye not only upon that particular front, but must be prepared to deal with a German offensive on other sections of the line. Nevertheless, just as soon as it was seen that the whole concentration of the German attack was directed upon that 5,000 yards of front, the British machine began to move. Troops could in safety be withdrawn from reserve, with the sure knowledge that no attack of any considerable proportions would be delivered at any other part of the line.

The wearied Canadians saw the end of their long trial approaching when, across the plain, leisurely and orderly, British troops were passing. Through the Canadian line came this gallant British brigade, and the reinforcements, old soldiers wise in war, who saw the remnants of the Canadian division sticking grimly to their task, cheered them lustily as they passed.

"It was our reward," wrote a Canadian soldier, "and of all the thrilling experiences we had had during those past two days, none was more thrilling than this splendid tribute which our comrades of the line gave us as they went forth to death to consolidate the work we had begun. I saw men who had come through that fight without the display of the slightest sign of emotion, trembling with pride as the soldiers of the Motherland passed, waving their hands cheerily, and singing their songs as though they were going out on a route march across Salisbury Plain, orderly, disciplined and magnificent."

That cheer was the tribute of the British Army to Canadian gallantry. It was something more, it was the first acknowledgment of the fellowship which now had been created. The Canadians had stood the test and had rung true, and in the roar of British cheering which swept across the bloody field to hearten the war- wearied men of Canada, came the first indication of the professional soldier's regard for Canadian valour.

Yet, though the British reinforcements had come up, and though the Canadians, heavy-footed, "sleeping as they walked," were being passed into reserve as battalion after battalion moved forward to relieve them, their work was not yet over. There was still a "hole" to be stopped, for the German attack had abated none of its vigour.

It was asking more than might reasonably be expected when the British general called upon Brigadier-General Curry for yet another effort. "Do you think your men could stand it?" he was asked, and the commander of the 2nd Brigade replied: "The men are tired, but they are ready and glad to go again to the trenches."

He did not speak without reason.

Never questioning the order, the Canadians turned about and went back to the firing line only a quarter of their original strength, but indomitable even in their weariness.

All Monday and Tuesday they held on to their line, and it was not until Wednesday—practically a week after the attack began—that they were relieved, and the tired men of Canada were sent back for their well-earned rest.

I have spoken only of the infantry and the part they played in that fight. Behind the infantry lines, however, the Canadian batteries were massed, and stuck to their posts, firing at close range and never losing a single gun. The final line taken by the Canadians and extended by the British and French, who had now re-organised and returned to the attack, was well south of St. Julien and north of the hamlet of Fortuin. From thence it curved down and up again to meet the Belgian right, and upon the Belgian fell no small amount of the honours of those sanguinary days.

The Belgian had been pushed from Lizerne; he had seen the Yser forced, and had himself been subjected to attacks delivered after the emission of gases; but he had come back with the vigour which we have always expected from the Belgian Army, and had carried Lizerne at the point of the bayonet.

The fight in that village was a prolonged and a terrible one. The Belgians brought their guns to close quarters and fired point-blank into the advancing German infantry, flinging the reinforcements back again across the Yser, and establishing a veritable curtain of shrapnel between the defenders of the village and all possible help; 600 German dead were picked up on the Lizerne front alone.

The second battle for Ypres had been, from the German point of view, much more successful than the first attack, since they had reduced the line to the left and had given themselves a new point from whence they might shell the town and its communications. The impartial estimate places the German losses in those successive attacks upon the Canadian front at from 12,000 to 15,000, but since the enemy occupied the ground on which those losses occurred, it is difficult to form an estimate. The Canadian losses were very heavy indeed. A statement issued by General Hughes, the Canadian Minister of Militia, gave a total of six thousand Canadian casualties between April 22 and April 30.

DESPATCHES RECEIVED FROM GENERAL FRENCH,
FEBRUARY 2—JUNE 15, 1915

Dispatch February 2nd

The following Despatch was received on February 12 by the Secretary of State for War from the Field-Marshal Commanding-in-Chief, The British Army in the Field:

General Headquarters,

February 2, 1915.

My Lord,

I have the honour to forward a further report on the operations of the Army under my command.

I. In the period under review the salient feature was the presence of His Majesty the King in the Field. His Majesty arrived at Headquarters on November 30, and left on December 5.

At a time when the strength and endurance of the troops had been tried to the utmost throughout the long and arduous Battle of Ypres-Armentières, the presence of His Majesty in their midst was of the greatest possible help and encouragement.

His Majesty visited all parts of the extensive area of operations, and held numerous inspections of the troops behind the line of trenches.

On November 16 Lieutenant His Royal Highness the Prince of Wales, K.G., Grenadier Guards, joined my Staff as Aide-de-Camp.

II. Since the date of my last report the operations of the Army under my command have been subject almost entirely to the limitations of weather.

History teaches us that the course of campaigns in Europe, which have been actively prosecuted during the months of December and January, have been largely influenced by weather conditions. It should, however, be thoroughly understood throughout the country that the most recent development of armaments and the latest methods of conducting warfare have added greatly to the difficulties and drawbacks of a vigorous winter campaign.

To cause anything more than a waste of ammunition long-range artillery fire requires constant and accurate observation; but this most necessary condition is rendered impossible of attainment in the midst of continual fog and mist.

Again, armies have now grown accustomed to rely largely on aircraft reconnaissance for accurate information of the enemy; but the effective performance of this service is materially influenced by wind and weather.

The deadly accuracy, range, and quick-firing capabilities of the modern rifle and machine gun require that a fire-swept zone be crossed in the shortest possible space of time by attacking troops. But if men are detained under the enemy's fire by the difficulty of emerging from a water-logged trench, and by the necessity of passing over ground knee-deep in holding mud and slush, such attacks become practically prohibitive owing to the losses they entail.

During the exigencies of the heavy fighting which ended in the last week of November the French and British Forces had become somewhat mixed up, entailing a certain amount of difficulty in matters of supply and in securing unity of command.

By the end of November I was able to concentrate the Army under my command in one area, and, by holding a shorter line, to establish effective reserves.

By the beginning of December there was a considerable falling off in the volume of artillery fire directed against our front by the enemy. Reconnaissance and reports showed that a certain amount of artillery had been withdrawn. We judged that the cavalry in our front, with the exception of one Division of the Guard, had disappeared.

There did not, however, appear to have been any great diminution in the numbers of infantry holding the trenches.

III. Although both artillery and rifle fire were exchanged with the enemy every day, and sniping went on more or less continuously during the hours of daylight, the operations which call for special record or comment are comparatively few.

During the last week in November some successful minor night operations were carried out in the 4th Corps.

On the night of November 23-24 a small party of the 2nd Lincolnshire Regiment, under Lieutenant E.H. Impey, cleared three of the enemy's advanced trenches opposite the 25th Brigade and withdrew without loss.

On the night of the 24th-25th Captain J.R. Minshull Ford, Royal Welsh Fusiliers, and Lieutenant E. L. Morris, Royal Engineers, with 15 men of the Royal Engineers and Royal Welsh Fusiliers, successfully mined and blew up a group of farms immediately in front of the German trenches on the Touquet-Bridoux Road which had been used by German snipers.

On the night of November 26-27 a small party of the 2nd Scots Guards, under Lieutenant Sir E. H. W. Hulse, Bt., rushed the trenches opposite the 20th Brigade; and after pouring a heavy fire into them returned with useful information as to the strength of the Germans and the position of machine guns.

The trenches opposite the 25th Brigade were rushed the same night by a patrol of the 2nd Rifle Brigade, under Lieutenant E. Durham.

On November 23 the 112th Regiment of the 14th German Army Corps succeeded in capturing some 800 yards of the trenches held by the Indian Corps, but the General Officer Commanding the Meerut Division organised a powerful counter- attack, which lasted throughout the night. At daybreak on November 24 the line was entirely re-established.

The operation was a costly one, involving many casualties, but the enemy suffered far more heavily. We captured over 100 prisoners, including 3 officers, as well as 3 machine guns and 2 trench mortars.

On December 7 the concentration of the Indian Corps was completed by the arrival of the Sirhind Brigade from Egypt.

On December 9 the enemy attempted to commence a strong attack against the 3rd Corps, particularly in front of the trenches held by the Argyll and Sutherland Highlanders and the Middlesex Regiment.

They were driven back with heavy loss, and did not renew the attempt. Our casualties were very slight.

During the early days of December certain indications along the whole front of the Allied Line induced the French Commanders and myself to believe that the enemy had withdrawn considerable forces from the Western Theatre.

Arrangements were made with the Commander of the 8th French Army for an attack to be commenced on the morning of December 14.

Operations began at 7 a.m. by a combined heavy artillery bombardment by the two French and the 2nd British Corps.

The British objectives were the Petit Bois and the Maedelsteed Spur, lying respectively to the west and south-west of the village of Wytschaete.

At 7.45 a.m. the Royal Scots, with great dash, rushed forward and attacked the former, while the Gordon Highlanders attacked the latter place.

The Royal Scots, commanded by Major F. J. Duncan, D.S.O., in face of a terrible machine-gun and rifle fire, carried the German trench on the west edge of the Petit Bois, capturing two machine guns and 53 prisoners, including one officer.

The Gordon Highlanders, with great gallantry, advanced up the Maedelsteed Spur, forcing the enemy to evacuate their front trench. They were, however, losing heavily, and found themselves unable to get any further. At nightfall they were obliged to fall back to their original position. Captain C. Boddam-Whetham and Lieutenant W. F. R. Dobie showed splendid dash, and with a few men entered the enemy's leading trenches; but they were all either killed or captured.

Lieutenant G. R. V. Hume-Gore and Lieutenant W. H. Paterson also distinguished themselves by their gallant leading.

Although not successful, the operation was most creditable to the fighting spirit of the Gordon Highlanders, most ably commanded by Major A. W. F. Baird, D.S.O.

As the 32nd French Division on the left had been unable to make any progress, the further advance of our infantry into the Wytschaete Wood was not practicable.

Possession of the western edge of the Petit Bois was, however, retained.

The ground was devoid of cover and so water-logged that a rapid advance was impossible, the men sinking deep in the mud at every step they took.

The artillery throughout the day was very skilfully handled by the C.R.A.'s of the 3rd, 4th, and 5th Divisions: Major-General F. D. V. Wing, C.B., Brigadier- General G. F. Milne, C.B., D.S.O., and Brigadier-General J. E. W. Headlam, C.B., D.S.O.

The casualties during the day were about 17 officers and 407 other ranks. The losses of the enemy were very considerable, large numbers of dead being found in the Petit Bois and also in the communicating trenches in front of the Gordon Highlanders, in one of which a hundred were counted by a night patrol.

On this day the artillery of the 4th Division, 3rd Corps, was used in support of the attack, under orders of the General Officer Commanding 2nd Corps.

The remainder of the 3rd Corps made demonstrations against the enemy with a view to preventing him from detaching troops to the area of operations of the 2nd Corps.

From December 15-17 the offensive operations which were commenced on the 14th were continued, but were confined chiefly to artillery bombardment.

The infantry advance against Wytschaete Wood was not practicable until the French on our left could make some progress to afford protection to that flank.

On the 17th it was agreed that the plan of attack as arranged should be modified; but I was requested to continue demonstrations along my line in order to assist and support certain French operations which were being conducted elsewhere.

IV. In his desire to act with energy up to his instructions to demonstrate and occupy the enemy, the General Officer Commanding the Indian Corps decided to take the advantage of what appeared to him a favourable opportunity to launch attacks against the advanced trenches in his front on December 18 and 19.

The attack of the Meerut Division on the left was made on the morning of the 19th with energy and determination, and was at first attended with considerable success, the enemy's advanced trenches being captured. Later on, however, a counter-attack drove them back to their original position with considerable loss.

The attack of the Lahore Division commenced at 4.30 a.m. It was carried out by two companies each of the 1st Highland Light Infantry and the 1st Battalion, 4th Gurkha Rifles, of the Sirhind Brigade, under Lieutenant-Colonel R. W. H. Ronaldson. This attack was completely successful, two lines of the enemy's trenches being captured with little loss.

Before daylight the captured trenches were filled with as many men as they would hold. The front was very restricted, communication to the rear impossible.

At daybreak it was found that the position was practically untenable. Both flanks were in the air, and a supporting attack, which was late in starting, and, therefore, conducted during daylight, failed; although attempted with the greatest gallantry and resolution.

Lieutenant-Colonel Ronaldson held on till dusk, when the whole of the captured trenches had to be evacuated, and the detachment fell back to its original line.

By the night of December 19 nearly all the ground gained during the day had been lost.

From daylight on December 20 the enemy commenced a heavy fire from artillery and trench mortars on the whole front of the Indian Corps. This was followed by infantry attacks, which were in especial force against Givenchy, and between that place and La Quinque Rue.

At about 10 a.m. the enemy succeeded in driving back the Sirhind Brigade, and capturing a considerable part of Givenchy, but the 57th Rifles and 9th Bhopals, north of the canal, and the Connaught Rangers, south of it, stood firm.

The 15th Sikhs of the Divisional Reserve were already supporting the Sirhind Brigade. On the news of the retirement of the latter being received, the 47th Sikhs were also sent up to reinforce General Brunker. The 1st Manchester Regiment, 4th Suffolk Regiment, and two battalions of French Territorials under General Carnegy were ordered to launch a vigorous counterattack from Pont Fixe through Givenchy to retake by a flank attack the trenches lost by the Sirhind Brigade.

Orders were sent to General Carnegy to divert his attack on Givenchy Village, and to re-establish the situation there.

A battalion of the 58th French Division was sent to Annequin in support.

About 5 p.m. a gallant attack by the 1st Manchester Regiment and one company of the 4th Suffolk Regiment had captured Givenchy, and had cleared the enemy out of the two lines of trenches to the North-East. To the east of the village the 9th Bhopal Infantry and 57th Rifles had maintained their positions, but the enemy were still in possession of our trenches to the north of the village.

General Macbean, with the Secunderabad Cavalry Brigade, 2nd Battalion, 8th Gurkha Rifles, and the 47th Sikhs, was sent up to support General Brunker, who at 2 p.m. directed General Macbean to move to a position of readiness in the second-line trenches from Maris northward, and to counter-attack vigorously if opportunity offered.

Some considerable delay appears to have occurred, and it was not until 1 a.m. on the 21st that the 47th Sikhs and the 7th Dragoon Guards under the command of Lieutenant-Colonel H. A. Lemprière, D.S.O., of the latter regiment, were launched in counter-attack.

They reached the enemy's trenches, but were driven out by enfilade fire, their gallant Commander being killed.

The main attack by the remainder of General Macbean's force, with the remnants of Lieutenant-Colonel Lemprière's detachment (which had again been rallied), was finally pushed in at about 4.30 a.m., and also failed.

In the northern section of the defensive line the retirement of the 2nd Battalion, 2nd Gurkha Rifles, at about 10 a.m. on the 20th, had left the flank of the 1st Seaforth Highlanders, on the extreme right of the Meerut Division line, much exposed. This battalion was left shortly afterwards completely in the air by the retirement of the Sirhind Brigade.

The 58th Rifles, therefore, were ordered to support the left of the Seaforth Highlanders, to fill the gap created by the retirement of the Gurkhas.

During the whole of the afternoon strenuous efforts were made by the Seaforth Highlanders to clear the trenches to their right and left. The 1st Battalion, 9th Gurkha Rifles, reinforced the 2nd Gurkhas near the orchard where the Germans were in occupation of the trenches abandoned by the latter regiment. The Garhwal Brigade was being very heavily attacked, and their trenches and loopholes were much damaged; but the brigade continued to hold its front and attack, connecting with the 6th Jats on the left of the Dehra Dun Brigade.

No advance in force was made by the enemy, but the troops were pinned to their ground by heavy artillery fire, the Seaforth Highlanders especially suffering heavily.

Shortly before nightfall the 2nd Royal Highlanders on the right of the Seaforth Highlanders had succeeded in establishing touch with the Sirhind Brigade; and the continuous line (though dented near the orchard) existed throughout the Meerut Division.

Early in the afternoon of December 20 orders were sent to the 1st Corps, which was then in general army reserve, to send an infantry brigade to support the Indian Corps.

The 1st Brigade was ordered to Bethune, and reached that place at midnight on December 20-21. Later in the day Sir Douglas Haig was ordered to move the whole of the 1st Division in support of the Indian Corps.

The 3rd Brigade reached Bethune between S a.m. and 9 a.m. on the 21st, and on the same date the 2nd Brigade arrived at Lacon at 1 p.m.

The 1 st Brigade was directed on Givenchy, via Pont Fixe, and the 3rd Brigade, through Gorre, on the trenches evacuated by the Sirhind Brigade.

The 2nd Brigade was directed to support; the Dehra Dun Brigade being placed at the disposal of the General Officer Commanding Meerut Division.

At 1 p.m. the General Officer Commanding 1st Division directed the 1st Brigade in attack from the west of Givenchy in a north-easterly direction, and the 3rd Brigade from Festubert in an east-north-easterly direction, the object being to pass the position originally held by us and to capture the German trenches 400 yards to the east of it.

By 5 p.m. the 1st Brigade had obtained a hold in Givenchy, and the ground south as far as the canal; and the 3rd Brigade had progressed to a point half a mile west of Festubert.

By nightfall the 1st South Wales Borderers and the 2nd Welsh Regiment of the 3rd Brigade had made a lodgment in the original trenches to the north-east of Festubert, the 1st Gloucestershire Regiment continuing the line southward along the track east of Festubert.

The 1st Brigade had established itself on the east side of Givenchy.

By 3 p.m. the 2nd Brigade was concentrated at Le Touret, and was ordered to retake the trenches which had been lost by the Dehra Dun Brigade.

By 10 p.m. the support trenches west of the orchard had been carried, but the original fire trenches had been so completely destroyed that they could not be occupied.

This operation was performed by the 1st Loyal North Lancashire Regiment and the 1st Northamptonshire Regiment, supported by the 2nd King's Royal Rifle Corps, in reserve.

Throughout this day the units of the Indian Corps rendered all the assistance and support they could in view of their exhausted condition.

At 1 p.m. on the 22nd Sir Douglas Haig took over command from Sir James Willcocks. The situation in the front line was then approximately as follows:—

South of the La Bassée Canal the Connaught Rangers of the Ferozepore Brigade had not been attacked. North of the canal a short length of our original line was still held by the 9th Bhopals and the 57th Rifles of the same brigade. Connecting with the latter was the 1st Brigade holding the village of Givenchy and its eastern and northern approaches. On the left of the 1st Brigade was the 3rd Brigade. Touch had been lost between the left of the former and the right of the latter. The 3rd Brigade held a line along, and in places advanced to, the east of the Festubert Road. Its left was in communication with the right of the Meerut Division line, where troops of the 2nd Brigade had just relieved the 1st Seaforth Highlanders. To the north, units of the 2nd Brigade held an indented line west of the orchard, connecting with half of the 2nd Royal Highlanders, half of the 41st Dogras and the 1st Battalion, 9th Gurkha Rifles. From this point to the north the 6th Jats and the whole of the Garhwal Brigade occupied the original line which they had held from the commencement of the operations.

The relief of most units of the southern sector was effected on the night of December 22. The Meerut Division remained under the orders of the 1st Corps, and was not completely withdrawn until December 27.

In the evening the position at Givenchy was practically re-established, and the 3rd Brigade had re-occupied the old line of trenches.

During the 23rd the enemy's activities ceased, and the whole position was restored to very much its original condition.

In my last despatch I had occasion to mention the prompt and ready help I received from the Lahore Division, under the command of Major-General H. B. B. Watkis, C.B., which was thrown into action immediately on arrival, when the British Forces were very hard pressed during the battle of Ypres-Armentières.

The Indian troops have fought with the utmost steadfastness and gallantry whenever they have been called upon.

Weather conditions were abnormally bad, the snow and floods precluding any active operations during the first three weeks of January.

V. At 7.30 a.m. on January 25 the enemy began to shell Bethune, and at 8 a.m. a strong hostile infantry attack developed south of the canal, preceded by a heavy bombardment of artillery, Minenwerfer and, possibly, the explosion of mines, though the latter is doubtful.

The British line south of the canal formed a pronounced salient from the canal on the left, hence running forward toward the railway triangle and back to the main La Bassée-Bethune Road, where it joined the French. This line was occupied by half a battalion of the Scots Guards, and half a battalion of the Coldstream Guards, of the 1st Infantry Brigade. The trenches in the salient were blown in almost at once; and the enemy's attack penetrated this line. Our troops retired to a partially prepared second line, running approximately due north and south from the canal to the road, some 500 yards west of the railway triangle. This second line had been strengthened by the construction of a keep half-way between the canal and the road. Here the other two half battalions of the above-mentioned regiments were in support.

These supports held up the enemy, who, however, managed to establish himself in the brick stacks and some communication trenches between the keep, the road and the canal—and even beyond and west of the keep on either side of it.

The London Scottish had in the meantime been sent up in support, and a counter- attack was organised with the 1st Royal Highlanders, part of the 1st Cameron Highlanders, and the 2nd King's Royal Rifle Corps, the latter regiment having been sent forward from the Divisional Reserve. The counter-attack was delayed in order to synchronise with a counter-attack north of the canal which was arranged for 1 p.m.

At 1 p.m. these troops moved forward, their flanks making good progress near the road and the canal, but their centre being held up. The 2nd Royal Sussex Regiment was then sent forward, late in the afternoon, to reinforce. The result was that the Germans were driven back far enough to enable a somewhat broken line to be taken up, running from the culvert on the railway, almost due south to the keep, and thence southeast to the main road.

The French left near the road had also been attacked and driven back a little, but not to so great an extent as the British right. Consequently, the French left was in advance of the British right and exposed to a possible flank attack from the north.

The Germans did not, however, persevere further in their attack.

The above-mentioned line was strengthened during the night, and the 1st Guards Brigade, which had suffered severely, was withdrawn into reserve and replaced by the 2nd Infantry Brigade. While this was taking place another, and equally severe, attack was delivered north of the canal against the village of Givenchy.

At 8.15 a.m., after a heavy artillery bombardment with high explosive shells, the enemy's infantry advanced under the effective fire of our artillery, which, however, was hampered by the constant interruption of telephonic communication between the observers and batteries. Nevertheless, our artillery fire, combined with that of the infantry in the fire trenches, had the effect of driving the enemy from his original direction of advance, with the result that his troops crowded together on the north-east corner of the village and broke through into the centre of the village as far as the keep, which had been previously put in a state of defence. The Germans had lost heavily, and a well-timed local counter- attack, delivered by the reserves of the 2nd Welsh Regiment and 1st South Wales Borderers, and by a company of the 1st Royal Highlanders (lent by the 1st Brigade as a working party—this company was at work on the keep at the time), was completely successful, with the result that, after about an hour's street fighting, all who had broken into the village were either captured or killed; and the original line round the village was re-established by noon.

South of the village, however, and close to the canal, the right of the 2nd Royal Munster Fusiliers fell back in conformity with the troops south of the canal; but after dark that regiment moved forward and occupied the old line.

During the course of the attack on Givenchy the enemy made five assaults on the salient at the north-east of the village about French Farm, but was repulsed every time with heavy loss.

V. On the morning of January 29 attacks were made on the right of the 1st Corps, south of the canal in the neighbourhood of La Bassée.

The enemy (part of the 14th German Corps), after a severe shelling, made a violent attack with scaling ladders on the keep, also to the north and south of it. In the keep and on the north side the Sussex Regiment held the enemy off, inflicting on him severe losses. On the south side the hostile infantry succeeded in reaching the Northamptonshire Regiment's trenches; but were immediately counter-attacked and all killed. Our artillery co-operated well with the infantry in repelling the attack.

In this action our casualties were inconsiderable, but the enemy lost severely, more than 200 of his killed alone being left in front of our position.

VI. On February 1 a fine piece of work was carried out by the 4th Brigade in the neighbourhood of Cuinchy.

Some of the 2nd Coldstream Guards were driven from their trenches at 2.30 a.m., but made a stand some twenty yards east of them in a position which they held till morning.

A counter-attack, launched at 3.15 a.m. by one company of the Irish Guards and half a company of the 2nd Coldstream Guards, proved unsuccessful, owing to heavy rifle fire from the east and south. At 10.5 a.m., acting under orders of the 1st Division, a heavy bombardment was opened on the lost ground for ten minutes; and this was followed immediately by an assault by about 50 men of the 2nd Coldstream Guards with bayonets, led by Captain A. Leigh Bennett, followed by 30 men of the Irish Guards, led by Second Lieutenant F. F. Graham, also with bayonets. These were followed by a party of Royal Engineers with sand bags and wire.

All the ground which had been lost was brilliantly retaken; the 2nd Coldstream Guards also taking another German trench and capturing two machine guns.

Thirty-two prisoners fell into our hands.

The General Officer Commanding 1st Division describes the preparation by the artillery as "splendid, the high explosive shells dropping in the exact spot with absolute precision."
In forwarding his report on this engagement, the General Officer Commanding First Army writes as follows:—

Special credit is due—

(i) To Major-General Haking, Commanding 1st Division, for the prompt manner in which he arranged this counter-attack, and for the general plan of action, which was crowned with success.

(ii) To the General Officer Commanding the 4th Brigade (Lord Cavan) for the thorough manner in which he carried out the orders of the General Officer Commanding the Division.

(iii) To the regimental officers, non-commissioned officers and men of the 2nd Coldstream Guards and Irish Guards, who, with indomitable pluck, stormed two sets of barricades, captured three German trenches, two machine guns, and killed or made prisoners many of the enemy.

VII. During the period under report the Royal Flying Corps has again performed splendid service. Although the weather was almost uniformly bad and the machines suffered from constant exposure, there have been only thirteen days on which no actual reconnaissance has been effected.

Approximately, one hundred thousand miles have been flown.

In addition to the daily and constant work of reconnaissance and co-operation with the artillery, a number of aerial combats have been fought, raids carried out, detrainments harassed, parks and petrol depôts bombed, etc.

Various successful bomb-dropping raids have been carried out, usually against the enemy's aircraft material. The principle of attacking hostile aircraft whenever and wherever seen (unless highly important information is being delivered) has been adhered to, and has resulted in the moral fact that enemy machines invariably beat immediate retreat when chased.

Five German aeroplanes are known to have been brought to the ground, and it would appear probable that others, though they have managed to reach their own lines, have done so in a considerably damaged condition.

VIII. In my despatch of November 20, 1914, 1 referred to the reinforcements of Territorial Troops which I had received, and I mentioned several units which had already been employed in the fighting line.

In the positions which I held for some years before the outbreak of this war I was brought into close contact with the Territorial Force, and I found every reason to hope and believe that, when the hour of trial arrived, they would justify every hope and trust which was placed in them.

The Lords Lieutenant of Counties and the Associations which worked under them bestowed a vast amount of labour and energy on the organisation of the Territorial Force; and I trust it may be some recompense to them to know that I, and the principal Commanders serving under me, consider that the Territorial Force has far more than justified the most sanguine hopes that any of us ventured to entertain of their value and use in the field. Commanders of Cavalry Divisions are unstinted in their praise of the manner in which the Yeomanry regiments attached to their brigades have done their duty, both in and out of action. The service of Divisional Cavalry is now almost entirely performed by Yeomanry, and Divisional Commanders report that they are very efficient.

Army Corps Commanders are loud in their praise of the Territorial Battalions which form part of nearly all the brigades at the front in the first line, and more than one of them have told me that these battalions are fast approaching, if they have not already reached, the standard of efficiency of Regular Infantry.

I wish to add a word about the Officers Training Corps. The presence of the Artists' Rifles (28th Battalion, The London Regiment) with the Army in France enabled me also to test the value of this organisation.

Having had some experience in peace of the working of the Officers Training Corps, I determined to turn the Artists' Rifles (which formed part of the Officers Training Corps in peace time) to its legitimate use. I therefore established the battalion as a Training Corps for Officers in the field.

The cadets pass through a course, which includes some thoroughly practical training as all cadets do a tour of 48 hours in the trenches, and afterwards write a report on what they see and notice. They also visit an observation post of a battery or group of batteries, and spend some hours there.

A Commandant has been appointed, and he arranges and supervises the work, sets schemes for practice, administers the school, delivers lectures, and reports on the candidates.

The cadets are instructed in all branches of military training suitable for platoon commanders. Machine-gun tactics, a knowledge of which is so necessary for all junior officers, is a special feature of the course of instruction.

When first started the school was able to turn out officers at the rate of 75 a month. This has since been increased to 100.

Reports received from Divisional and Army Corps Commanders on officers who have been trained at the school are most satisfactory.

IX. Since the date of my last report I have been able to make a close personal inspection of all the units in the command. I was most favourably impressed by all I saw.

The troops composing the Army in France have been subjected to as severe a trial as it is possible to impose upon any body of men. The desperate fighting described in my last despatch had hardly been brought to a conclusion when they were called upon to face the rigours and hardships of a winter campaign. Frost and snow have alternated with periods of continuous rain.

The men have been called upon to stand for many hours together almost up to their waists in bitterly cold water, only separated by one or two hundred yards from a most vigilant enemy. Although every measure which science and medical knowledge could suggest to mitigate these hardships was employed, the sufferings of the men have been very great.

In spite of all this they presented, at the inspections to which I have referred, a most soldier-like, splendid, though somewhat war-worn appearance. Their spirit remains high and confident; their general health is excellent, and their condition most satisfactory.

I regard it as most unfortunate that circumstances have prevented any account of many splendid instances of courage and endurance, in the face of almost unparalleled hardship and fatigue in war, coming regularly to the knowledge of the public.

Reinforcements have arrived from England with remarkable promptitude and rapidity. They have been speedily drafted' into the ranks, and most of the units I inspected were nearly complete when I saw them. In appearance and quality the drafts sent out have exceeded my most sanguine expectations, and I consider the Army in France is much indebted to the Adjutant-General's Department at the War Office for the efficient manner in which its requirements have been met in this most essential respect.

With regard to these inspections, I may mention in particular the fine appearance presented by the 27th and 28th Divisions, composed principally of battalions which had come from India. Included in the former division was the Princess Patricia's Royal Canadian Regiment. They are a magnificent set of men, and have since done excellent work in the trenches.

It was some three weeks after the events recorded in paragraph 4 that I made my inspection of the Indian Corps, under Sir James Willcocks. The appearance they presented was most satisfactory, and fully confirmed my first opinion that the Indian troops only required rest, and a little acclimatising, to bring out all their fine inherent fighting qualities.

I saw the whole of the Indian Cavalry Corps, under Lieutenant-General Rimington, on a mounted parade soon after their arrival. They are a magnificent body of Cavalry, and will, I feel sure, give the best possible account of themselves when called upon.

In the meantime, at their own particular request, they have taken their turn in the trenches, and performed most useful and valuable service.

X. The Rt. Rev. Bishop Taylor Smith, C.V.O., D.D., Chaplain-General to the Forces, arrived at my Headquarters on January 6, on a tour of inspection throughout the command.

The Cardinal Archbishop of Westminster has also visited most of the Irish Regiments at the front and the principal centres on the line of communications.

In a quiet and unostentatious manner the chaplains of all denominations have worked with devotion and energy in their respective spheres.

The number with the forces in the field at the commencement of the war was comparatively small, but towards the end of last year the Rev. J. M. Simms, D.D., K.H.C., Principal Chaplain, assisted by his Secretary, the Rev. W. Drury, reorganised the branch, and placed the spiritual welfare of the soldier on a more satisfactory footing. It is hoped that the further increase of personnel may be found possible.

I cannot speak too highly of the devoted manner in which all chaplains, whether with the troops in the trenches, or in attendance on the sick and wounded in casualty clearing stations and hospitals on the line of communications, have worked throughout the campaign.

Since the commencement of hostilities the work of the Royal Army Medical Corps has been carried out with untiring zeal, skill, and devotion. Whether at the front under conditions such as obtained during the fighting on the Aisne, when casualties were heavy and accommodation for their reception had to be improvised, or on the line of communications, where an average of some 11,000 patients have been daily under treatment, the organisation of the Medical Services has always been equal to the demands made upon it.

The careful system of sanitation introduced into the Army has, with the assistance of other measures, kept the troops free from any epidemic, in support of which it is to be noticed that since the commencement of the war some 500 cases only of enteric have occurred.

The organisation for the first time in war of Motor Ambulance Convoys is due to the initiative and organising powers of Surgeon-General T. J. O'Donnell, D.S.O., ably assisted by Major P. Evans, Royal Army Medical Corps.

Two of these convoys, composed entirely of Red Cross Society personnel have done excellent work under the superintendence of Regular Medical Officers.

Twelve Hospital Trains ply between the front and the various bases. I have visited several of the trains when halted in stations, and have found them conducted with great comfort and efficiency. During the more recent phase of the campaign the creation of Rest Depôts at the front has materially reduced the wastage of men to the line of communications.

Since the latter part of October, 1914, the whole of the medical arrangements have been in the hands of Surgeon-General Sir A. T. Sloggett, C.M.G., K.H.S., under whom Surgeon-General T. P. Woodhouse and Surgeon-General T. J. O'Donnell have been responsible for the organisation on the line of communications and at the front respectively.

XI. The exceptional and peculiar conditions brought about by the weather have caused large demands to be made upon the resources and skill of the Royal Engineers.

Every kind of expedient has had to be thought out and adopted to keep the lines of trenches and defence work effective.

The Royal Engineers have shown themselves as capable of overcoming the ravages caused by violent rain and floods as they have been throughout in neutralising the effect of the enemy's artillery. In this connection I wish particularly to mention the excellent services performed by my Chief Engineer, Brigadier-General G. H. Fowke, who has been indefatigable in supervising all such work. His ingenuity and skill have been most valuable in the local construction of the various expedients which experience has shown to be necessary in prolonged trench warfare.

XII. I have no reason to modify in any material degree my views of the general military situation as expressed in my dispatch of November 20, 1914.

XIII. I have once more gratefully to acknowledge the valuable help and support I have received throughout this period from General Foch, General D'Urbal, and General Maud'huy of the French Army.

I have the honour to be,
Your Lordship's most obedient Servant,
J. D. P. French, Field-Marshal,
Commanding-in-Chief, The British Army in the Field.

Dispatch April 5th

The following Despatch has been received by the Secretary of State for War from the Field-Marshal Commanding-in-Chief, the British Army in the Field:

General Headquarters,

April 5, 1915.

My Lord,

I have the honour to report the operations of the Forces under my command since the date of my last dispatch, February 2, 1915.

I. The event of chief interest and importance which has taken place is the victory achieved over the enemy at the Battle of Neuve Chapelle, which was fought on March 10, 11, and 12. The main attack was delivered by troops of the First Army under the command of General Sir Douglas Haig, supported by a large force of Heavy Artillery, a Division of Cavalry, and some Infantry "of the general reserve."

Secondary and holding attacks and demonstrations were made along the front of the Second Army under the direction of its Commander, General Sir Horace Smith- Dorrien.

Whilst the success attained was due to the magnificent bearing and indomitable courage displayed by the troops of the 4th and Indian Corps, I consider that the able and skilful dispositions which were made by the General Officer Commanding First Army contributed largely to the defeat of the enemy and to the capture of his position. The energy and vigour with which General Sir Douglas Haig handled his command show him to be a leader of great ability and power.

Another action of considerable importance was brought about by a surprise attack of the Germans made on March 14 against the 27th Division holding the trenches east of St. Éloi. A large force of artillery was concentrated in this area under cover of mist, and a heavy volume of fire was suddenly brought to bear on the trenches at 5 p.m. This artillery attack was accompanied by two mine explosions; and, in the confusion caused by these and the suddenness of the attack, the position of St. Éloi was captured and held for some hours by the enemy.

Well-directed and vigorous counter-attacks, in which the troops of the 5th Army Corps showed great bravery and determination, restored the situation by the evening of the 15th.

A more detailed account of these operations will appear in subsequent pages of this despatch.
II. On February 6 a brilliant action by troops of the 1st Corps materially improved our position in the area south of the La Bassée Canal. During the previous night parties of Irish Guards and of the 3rd Battalion Coldstream Guards had succeeded in gaining ground whence converging fire could be directed on the flanks and rear of certain "brick-stacks" occupied by the Germans, which had been for some time a source of considerable annoyance.

At 2 p.m. the affair commenced with a severe bombardment of the "brick- stacks" and the enemy's trenches. A brisk attack by the 3rd Coldstream Guards and Irish Guards from our trenches west of the "brick-stacks" followed, and was supported by fire from the flanking positions which had been seized the previous night by the same regiments. The attack succeeded, the 44 brick-stacks "were occupied without difficulty, and a line established north and south through a point about forty yards east of the 44 brick-stacks."

The casualties suffered by the 5th Corps throughout the period under review, and particularly during the month of February, have been heavier than those in other parts of the line. I regret this; but I do not think, taking all the circumstances into consideration, that they were unduly numerous. The position then occupied by the 5th Corps has always been a very vulnerable part of our line; the ground is marshy, and trenches are most difficult to construct and maintain. The 27th and 28th Divisions of the 5th Corps have had no previous experience of European warfare, and a number of the units composing it had only recently returned from service in tropical climates. In consequence, the hardships of a rigorous winter campaign fell with greater weight upon these Divisions than upon any other in the command.

Chiefly owing to these causes, the 5th Corps, up to the beginning of March, was constantly engaged in counter-attack to retake trenches and ground which had been lost.

In their difficult and arduous task, however, the troops displayed the utmost gallantry and devotion; and it is most creditable to the skill and energy of their leaders that I am able to report how well they have surmounted all their difficulties, that the ground first taken over by them is still intact, and held with little greater loss than is incurred by troops in all other parts of the line.

On February 14 the 82nd Brigade of the 27th Division was driven from its trenches east of St. Éloi; but by 7 a.m. on the 15th all these trenches had been recaptured, fifteen prisoners taken, and sixty German dead counted in front of the trenches. Similarly in the 28th Division trenches were lost by the 85th Brigade and retaken the following night.

During the month of February the enemy made several attempts to get through all along the line, but he was invariably repulsed with loss. A particularly vigorous attempt was made on February 17 against the trenches held by the Indian Corps, but it was brilliantly repulsed.

On February 28 a successful minor attack was made on the enemy's trenches near St. Éloi by small parties of the Princess Patricia's Canadian Light Infantry. The attack was divided into three small groups, the whole under the command of Lieutenant Crabbe: No. 1 Group under Lieutenant Papineau, No. 2 Group under Sergeant Patterson, and No. 3 Group under Company Sergeant-Major Lloyd.

The head of the party got within fifteen or twenty yards of the German trench and charged; it was dark at the time (about 5.15 a.m.).

Lieutenant Crabbe, who showed the greatest dash and élan, took his party over everything in the trench until they had gone down it about eighty yards, when they were stopped by a barricade of sandbags and timber. This party, as well as the others, then pulled down the front face of the German parapet. A number of Germans were killed and wounded, and a few prisoners were taken. The services performed by this distinguished corps have continued to be very valuable since I had occasion to refer to them in my last despatch. They have been most ably organised, trained, and commanded by Lieutenant-Colonel F. D. Farquhar, D.S.O., who, I deeply regret to say, was killed while superintending some trench work on March 20. His loss will be deeply felt.

A very gallant attack was made by the 4th Battalion of the King's Royal Rifle Corps of the 80th Brigade on the enemy's trenches in the early hours of March 2. The Battalion was led by Major Widdrington, who launched it at 12.30 a.m. (he himself being wounded during its progress), covered by an extremely accurate and effective artillery fire. About sixty yards of the enemy's trench were cleared, but the attack was brought to a standstill by a very strong barricade, in attempting to storm which several casualties were incurred.

III. During the month of February I arranged with General Foch to render the 9th French Corps, holding the trenches on my left, some much-needed rest by sending the three Divisions of the British Cavalry Corps to hold a portion of the French trenches, each division for a period of ten days alternately.

It was very gratifying to me to note once again in this campaign the eager readiness which the Cavalry displayed to undertake a role which does not properly belong to them in order to support and assist their French comrades.

In carrying out this work leaders, officers, and men displayed the same skill and energy which I have had reason to comment upon in former despatches.

The time passed by the Cavalry in the French trenches was, on the whole, quiet and uneventful, but there are one or two incidents calling for remark.

At about 1.45 a.m. on February 16 a half-hearted attack was made against the right of the line held by the 2nd Cavalry Division, but it was easily repulsed by rifle fire, and the enemy left several dead in front of the trenches. The attack was delivered against the second and third trenches from the right of the line of this Division.

At 6 a.m. on the 21st the enemy blew up one of the 2nd Cavalry Division trenches, held by the 16th Lancers, and some adjoining French trenches. The enemy occupied forty yards of our trench and tried to advance, but were stopped. An immediate counter-attack by the supporting squadron was stopped by machine-gun fire. The line was established opposite the gap, and a counterattack by two squadrons and one company of French reserve was ordered. At 5.30 p.m. 2nd Cavalry Division reported that the counter-attack did not succeed in re-taking the trench blown in, but that a new line had been established forty yards in rear of it, and that there was no further activity on the part of the enemy. At 10 p.m. the situation was unchanged.

The Commander of the Indian Cavalry Corps expressed a strong desire that the troops under his command should gain some experience in trench warfare. Arrangements were made, therefore, with the General Officer Commanding the Indian Corps, in pursuance of which the various units of the Indian Cavalry Corps have from time to time taken a turn in the trenches, and have thereby gained some valuable experience.

IV. About the end of February many vital considerations induced me to believe that a vigorous offensive movement by the Forces under my command should be planned and carried out at the earliest possible moment.

Amongst the more important reasons which convinced me of this necessity were:— The general aspect of the Allied situation throughout Europe, and particularly the marked success of the Russian Army in repelling the violent onslaughts of Marshal von Hindenburg; the apparent weakening of the enemy in my front, and the necessity for assisting our Russian Allies to the utmost by holding as many hostile troops as possible in the Western Theatre; the efforts to this end which were being made by the French Forces at Arras and Champagne; and, perhaps the most weighty consideration of all, the need of fostering the offensive spirit in the troops under my command after the trying and possibly enervating experiences which they had gone through of a severe winter in the trenches. In a former despatch I commented upon the difficulties and drawbacks which the winter weather in this climate imposes upon a vigorous offensive. Early in March these difficulties became greatly lessened by the drying up of the country and by spells of brighter weather.

I do not propose in this despatch to enter at length into the considerations which actuated me in deciding upon the plan, time, and place of my attack, but Your Lordship is fully aware of these. As mentioned above, the main attack was carried out by units of the First Army, supported by troops of the Second Army and the general reserve.

The object of the main attack was to be the capture of the village of Neuve Chapelle and the enemy's position at that point, and the establishment of our line as far forward as possible to the east of that place.

The object, nature, and scope of the attack, and instructions for the conduct of the operation were communicated by me to Sir Douglas Haig in a secret memorandum dated February 19. The main topographical feature of this part of the theatre is a marked ridge which runs south-west from a point two miles south-west of Lille to the village of Fournes, whence two spurs run out, one due west to a height known as Haut Pommereau, the other following the line of the main road to Lilies.

The buildings of the village of Neuve Chapelle run along the Rue du Bois- Fauquisart Road. There is a triangle of roads just north of the village. This area consists of a few big houses, with walls, gardens, orchards, etc., and here, with the aid of numerous machine-guns, the enemy had established a strong post which flanked the approaches to the village.

The Bois du Biez, which lies roughly south-east of the village of Neuve Chapelle, influenced the course of this operation.

Full instructions as to assisting and supporting the attack were issued to the Second Army. The battle opened at 7.30 a.m. on March 10 by a powerful artillery bombardment of the enemy's position at Neuve Chapelle. The artillery bombardment had been well prepared and was most effective, except on the extreme northern portion of the front of attack.

At 8.5 a.m. the 23rd (left) and 25th (right) Brigades of the 8th Division assaulted the German trenches on the north-west of the village.

At the same hour the Garhwal Brigade of the Meerut Division, which occupied the position to the south of Neuve Chapelle, assaulted the German trenches in its front.

The Garhwal Brigade and the 25th Brigade carried the enemy's lines of entrenchments where the wire entanglements had been almost entirely swept away by our shrapnel fire. The 23rd Brigade, however, on the northeast, was held up by the wire entanglements, which were not sufficiently cut. At 8.5 a.m. the artillery turned on to Neuve Chapelle, and at 8.35 a.m. the advance of the infantry was continued.

The 25th and Garhwal Brigades pushed on eastward and north-eastward respectively, and succeeded in getting a footing in the village. The 23rd Brigade was still held up in front of the enemy's wire entanglements, and could not progress. Heavy losses were suffered, especially in the Middlesex Regiment and the Scottish Rifles. The progress, however, of the 25th Brigade into Neuve Chapelle immediately to the south of the 23rd Brigade had the effect of turning the southern flank of the enemy's defences in front of the 23rd Brigade.

This fact, combined with powerful artillery support, enabled the 23rd Brigade to get forward between 10 and 11 a.m., and by 11 a.m. the whole of the village of Neuve Chapelle and the roads leading northward and south-westward from the eastern end of that village were in our hands. During this time our artillery completely cut off the village and the surrounding country from any German reinforcements which could be thrown into the fight to restore the situation by means of a curtain of shrapnel fire. Prisoners subsequently reported that all attempts at reinforcing the front line were checked.

Steps were at once taken to consolidate the position won.

Considerable delay occurred after the capture of the Neuve Chapelle position. The infantry was greatly disorganised by the violent nature of the attack and by its passage through the enemy's trenches and the buildings of the village. It was necessary to get units to some extent together before pushing on. The telephonic communication being cut by the enemy's fire rendered communication between front and rear most difficult. The fact of the left of the 23rd Brigade having been held up had kept back the 8th Division, and had involved a portion of the 25th Brigade in fighting to the north out of its proper direction of advance. All this required adjustment. An orchard held by the enemy north of Neuve Chapelle also threatened the flank of an advance towards the Aubers Ridge.

I am of opinion that this delay would not have occurred had the clearly expressed order of the General Officer Commanding First Army been more carefully observed.

The difficulties above enumerated might have been overcome at an earlier period of the day if the General Officer Commanding 4th Corps had been able to bring his reserve brigades more speedily into action.

As it was, the further advance did not commence before 3.30 p.m.
The 21st Brigade was able to form up in the open on the left without a shot being fired at it, thus showing that at the time the enemy's resistance had been paralysed. The Brigade pushed forward in the direction of Moulin de Piètre.

At first it made good progress, but was subsequently held up by the machine- gun fire from the houses and from a defended work in the line of the German entrenchments opposite the right of the 22nd Brigade.

Further to the south the 24th Brigade, which had been directed on Piètre, was similarly held up by machine-guns in the houses and trenches at the road junction six hundred yards north-west of Piètre.

The 25th Brigade, on the right of the 24th, was also held up by machine-guns from a bridge held by the Germans, over the River des Layes, which is situated to the north-west of the Bois Du Biez. Whilst two Brigades of the Meerut Division were establishing themselves on the new line, the Dehra Dun Brigade, supported by the Jullundur Brigade of the Lahore Division, moved to the attack of the Bois Du Biez, but were held up on the line of the River Des Layes by the German post at the bridge which enfiladed them and brought them to a standstill.

The defended bridge over the River Des Layes and its neighbourhood immediately assumed considerable importance. Whilst artillery fire was brought to bear, as far as circumstances would permit, on this point, Sir Douglas Haig directed the 1st Corps to dispatch one or more battalions of the 1st Brigade in support of the troops attacking the bridge. Three battalions were thus sent to Richebourg St. Vaast. Darkness coming on, and the enemy having brought up reinforcements, no further progress could be made, and the Indian Corps and 4th Corps proceeded to consolidate the position they had gained.

Whilst the operations which I have thus briefly recorded were going on, the 1st Corps, in accordance with orders, delivered an attack in the morning from Givenchy, simultaneously with that against Neuve Chapelle; but, as the enemy's wire was insufficiently cut, very little progress could be made, and the troops at this point did little more than hold fast the Germans in front of them.
On the following day, 11 March, the attack was renewed by the 4th and Indian Corps, but it was soon seen that a further advance would be impossible until the artillery had dealt effectively with the various houses and defended localities which held up the troops along the entire front. Efforts were made to direct the artillery fire accordingly; but owing to the weather conditions, which did not permit of aerial observation, and the fact that nearly all the telephonic communications between the artillery observers and their batteries had been cut, it was impossible to do so with sufficient accuracy. Even when our troops which were pressing forward occupied a house here and there, it was not possible to stop our artillery fire, and the infantry had to be withdrawn.
The two principal points which barred the advance were the same as on the preceding day—namely, the enemy's position about Moulin de Piètre and at the bridge over the River des Layes.
On March 12 the same unfavourable conditions as regards weather prevailed, and hampered artillery action.

Although the 4th and Indian Corps most gallantly attempted to capture the strongly fortified positions in their front, they were unable to maintain themselves, although they succeeded in holding them for some hours.

Operations on this day were chiefly remarkable for the violent counter- attacks, supported by artillery, which were delivered by the Germans, and the ease with which they were repulsed.
As most of the objects for which the operations had been undertaken had been attained, and as there were reasons why I considered it inadvisable to continue the attack at that time, I directed Sir Douglas Haig on the night of the 12th to hold and consolidate the ground which had been gained by the 4th and Indian Corps, and to suspend further offensive operations for the present.

On the morning of the 12th I informed the General Officer Commanding 1st Army that he could call on the 2nd Cavalry Division, under General Gough, for immediate support in the event of the successes of the First Army opening up opportunities for its favourable employment.

This Division and a Brigade of the North Midland Division, which was temporarily attached to it, was moved forward for this purpose.

The 5th Cavalry Brigade, under Sir Philip Chetwode, reached the Rue Bacquerot at 4 p.m. with a view to rendering immediate support; but he was informed by the General Officer Commanding 4th Corps that the situation was not so favourable as he had hoped it would be, and that no further action by the cavalry was advisable.

General Gough's command, therefore, retired to Estaires.

The artillery of all kinds was handled with the utmost energy and skill, and rendered invaluable support in the prosecution of the attack.

The losses during these three days' fighting were, I regret to say, very severe, numbering—
190 officers and 2,337 other ranks, killed.
359 officers and 8,174 other ranks, wounded.
23 officers and 1,728 other ranks, missing.

But the results attained were, in my opinion, wide and far-reaching.

The enemy left several thousand dead on the battlefield, which were seen and counted; and we have positive information that upwards of 12,000 wounded were removed to the north-east and east by train.

Thirty officers and 1,657 other ranks of the enemy were captured.

I can best express my estimate of this battle by quoting an extract from a Special Order of the Day which I addressed to Sir Douglas Haig and the first Army at its conclusion:—

"I am anxious to express to you personally my warmest appreciation of the skilful manner in which you have carried out your orders, and my fervent and most heartfelt appreciation of the magnificent gallantry and devoted, tenacious courage displayed by all ranks whom you have ably led to success and victory."

V. Some operations in the nature of holding attacks, carried out by troops of the Second Army, were instrumental in keeping the enemy in front of them occupied, and preventing reinforcements being sent from those portions of the front to the main point of attack.

At 12.30 a.m. on March 12 the 17th Infantry Brigade of the 4th Division, 3rd Corps, engaged in an attack on the enemy which resulted in the capture of the village of L'Épinette and adjacent farms. Supported by a brisk fire from the 18th Infantry Brigade, the 17th Infantry Brigade, detailed for the attack, assaulted in two columns converging, and obtained the first houses of the village without much loss. The remainder of the village was very heavily wired, and the enemy got away by means of communication trenches while our men were cutting through the wire.

The enemy suffered considerable loss; our casualties being five officers and 30 other ranks killed and wounded.

The result of this operation was that an advance of 300 yards was made on a front of half a mile. All attempts to retake this position have been repulsed with heavy loss to the enemy.

The General Officer Commanding the Second Corps arranged for an attack on a part of the enemy's position to the south-west of the village of Wytschaete which he had timed to commence at 10 a.m. on March 12. Owing to dense fog, the assault could not be made until 4 o'clock in the afternoon. It was then commenced by the Wiltshire and Worcestershire Regiments, but was so hampered by the mist and the approach of darkness that nothing more was effected than holding the enemy to his ground.

The action of St. Éloi referred to in the first paragraph of this despatch commenced at 5 p.m. on March 14 by a very heavy cannonade which was directed against our trenches in front of St. Éloi, the village itself, and the approaches to it. There is a large mound lying to the south-east of the village. When the artillery attack was at its height a mine was exploded under this mound, and a strong hostile infantry attack was immediately launched against the trenches and the mound.

Our artillery opened fire at once, as well as our infantry, and inflicted considerable losses on the enemy during their advance; but, chiefly owing to the explosion of the mine and the surprise of the overwhelming artillery attack, the enemy's infantry had penetrated the first line of trenches at some points. As a consequence the garrisons of other works which had successfully resisted the assault were enfiladed and forced to retire just before it turned dark.

A counter-attack was at once organised by the General Officer Commanding 82nd Brigade, under the orders of the General Officer Commanding 27th Division, who brought up a reserve brigade to support it.

The attack was launched at 2 a.m., and the 82nd Brigade succeeded in recapturing the portion of the village of St. Éloi which was in the hands of the enemy and a portion of the trenches east of it. At 3 a.m. the 80th Brigade in support took more trenches to the east and west of the village.

The counter-attack, which was well carried out under difficult conditions, resulted in the recapture of all lost ground of material importance.

It is satisfactory to be able to record that, though the troops occupying the first line of trenches were at first overwhelmed, they afterwards behaved very gallantly in the counter-attack for the recovery of the lost ground; and the following units earned and received the special commendation of the Army Commander:—The 2nd Royal Irish Fusiliers, the 2nd Duke of Cornwall's Light Infantry, the 1st Leinster Regiment, the 4th Rifle Brigade, and the Princess Patricia's Canadian Light Infantry. A vigorous attack made by the enemy on the 17th to recapture these trenches was repulsed with great loss.

Throughout the period under review night enterprises by smaller or larger patrols, which were led with consummate skill and daring, have been very active along the whole line.

A moral superiority has thus been established, and valuable information has been collected. I cannot speak too highly of the invincible courage and the remarkable resource displayed by these patrols.

The troops of the 3rd Corps have particularly impressed me by their conduct of these operations.

VI. The work of the Royal Flying Corps throughout this period, and especially during the operations of 10, 11, and 12 March, was of the greatest value. Though the weather on 10 March and on the subsequent days was very unfavourable for aerial work, on account of low-lying clouds and mist, a remarkable number of hours' flying of a most valuable character were effected, and continuous and close reconnaissance was maintained over the enemy's front.

In addition to the work of reconnaissance and observation of artillery fire, the Royal Flying Corps was charged with the special duty of hampering the enemy's movements by destroying various points on his communications. The railways at Menin, Courtrai, Don, and Douai were attacked, and it is known that very extensive damage was effected at certain of these places. Part of a troop train was hit by a bomb, a wireless installation near Lille is believed to have been effectively destroyed, and a house in which the enemy had installed one of his Headquarters was set on fire. These afford other instances of successful operations of this character. Most of the objectives mentioned were attacked at a height of only 100 to 150 feet. In one case the pilot descended to about 50 feet above the point he was attacking.

Certain new and important forms of activity, which it is undesirable to specify, have been initiated and pushed forward with much vigour and success.

There have been only eight days during the period under review on which reconnaissances have not been made. A total of approximately 130,000 miles have been flown—almost entirely over the enemy's lines.

No great activity has been shown over our troops on the part of the enemy's aircraft, but they have been attacked whenever and wherever met with, and usually forced down or made to seek refuge in their own lines.

VII. In my last despatch I referred to the remarkable promptitude and rapidity with which reinforcements arrived in this country from England. In connection with this it is of interest to call attention to the fact that, in spite of the heavy casualties incurred in the fighting between 10 and 15 March, all deficiencies, both in officers and rank and file, were made good within a few days of the conclusion of the battle.

The drafts for the Indian Contingents have much improved of late, and are now quite satisfactory. Since the date of my last report the general health of the Army has been excellent; enteric has decreased, and there has been no recurrence on any appreciable scale of the "foot" trouble which appeared so threatening in December and January.

These results are due to the skill and energy which have characterised in a marked degree the work of the Royal Army Medical Corps throughout the campaign, under the able supervision of Surgeon-General T. J. O'Donnell, D.S.O., Deputy Director-General, Medical Services. But much credit is also due to Divisional, Brigade, Regimental, and Company Commanders for the close supervision which has been kept over the health of their men by seeing that the precautions laid down for the troops before entering and after leaving the trenches are duly observed, and by the establishment and efficient maintenance of bathing-places and wash-houses, and by the ingenious means universally employed throughout the Forces to maintain the cleanliness of the men, having regard both to their bodies and their clothing.

I have inspected most of these houses and establishments, and consider them models of careful organisation and supervision.

I would particularly comment upon the energy displayed by the Royal Army Medical Corps in the scientific efforts they have made to discover and check disease in its earliest stages by a system of experimental research, which I think has never before been so fully developed in the field..

In this work they have been ably assisted by those distinguished members of the medical profession who are now employed as Military Medical Officers, and whose invaluable services I gratefully acknowledge.

The actual strength of the Force in the field has been increased and the health of the troops improved by a system of "convalescent" hospitals.

In these establishments slight wounds and minor ailments are treated, and men requiring attention and rest are received.

By these means efficient soldiers, whose services would otherwise be lost for a long time, are kept in the country, whilst a large number of men are given immediate relief and rest when they require it without removing them from the area of operations.

This adds materially to the fighting efficiency of the Forces.

The principal convalescent hospital is at St. Omer. It was started and organised by Colonel A. F. L. Bate, Army Medical Service, whose zeal, energy, and organising power have rendered it a model hospital of its kind, and this example has materially assisted in the efficient organisation of similar smaller establishments at every Divisional Headquarters.

VIII. I have already commented upon the number and severity of the casualties in action which have occurred in the period under report. Here once again I have to draw attention to the excellent work done by Surgeon-General O'Donnell and his officers. No organisation could excel the efficiency of the arrangements—whether in regard to time, space, care and comfort, or transport—which are made for the speedy evacuation of the wounded.

I wish particularly to express my deep sense of the loss incurred by the Army in general and by the Forces in France in particular, in the death of Brigadier- General J. E. Gough, V.C., C.M.G., A.D.C., late Brigadier-General, General Staff, First Army, which occurred on 22 February, as a result of a severe wound received on 20 February when inspecting the trenches of the 4th Corps.

I always regarded General Gough as one of our most promising military leaders of the future. His services as a Staff Officer throughout the campaign have been invaluable, and I had already brought his name before Your Lordship for immediate promotion.

I can well understand how deeply these casualties are felt by the nation at large, but each daily report shows clearly that they are being endured on at least an equal scale by all the combatants engaged throughout Europe, friends and foes alike.

In war as it is to-day between civilised nations, armed to the teeth with the present deadly rifle and machine-gun, heavy casualties are absolutely unavoidable. For the slightest undue exposure the heaviest toll is exacted.

The power of defence conferred by modern weapons is the main cause of the long duration of the battles of the present day, and it is this fact which mainly accounts for such loss and waste of life. Both one and the other can, however, be shortened and lessened if attacks can be supported by the most efficient and powerful force of artillery available; but an almost unlimited supply of ammunition is necessary and a most liberal discretionary power as to its use must be given to the Artillery Commanders.

I am confident that this is the only means by which great results can be obtained with a minimum of loss.

IX. On February 15 the Canadian Division began to arrive in this country. I inspected the Division, which was under the command of Lieutenant-General E. A. H. Alderson, C.B., on February 20. They presented a splendid and most soldier-like appearance on parade. The men were of good physique, hard and fit. I judged by what I saw of them that they were well trained and quite able to take their places in the line of battle.

Since then the Division has thoroughly justified the good opinion I formed of it.

The troops of the Canadian Division were first attached for a few days by brigades for training in the 3rd Corps trenches under Lieutenant-General Sir William Pulteney, who gave me such an excellent report of their efficiency that I was able to employ them in the trenches early in March.

During the Battle of Neuve Chapelle they held a part of the line allotted to the First Army, and, although they were not actually engaged in the main attack, they rendered valuable help by keeping the enemy actively employed in front of their trenches.

All the soldiers of Canada serving in the Army under my command have so far splendidly upheld the traditions of the Empire, and will, I feel sure, prove to be a great source of additional strength to the forces in this country.

In former despatches I have been able to comment very favourably upon the conduct and bearing of the Territorial Forces throughout the operations in which they have been engaged.

As time goes on, and I see more and more of their work, whether in the trenches or engaged in more active operations, I am still further impressed with their value.

Several battalions were engaged in the most critical moments of the heavy fighting which occurred in the middle of March, and they acquitted themselves with the utmost credit.

Up till lately the troops of the Territorial Forces in this country were only employed by battalions, but for some weeks past I have seen formed divisions working together, and I have every hope that their employment in the larger units will prove as successful as in the smaller.

These opinions are fully borne out by the result of the close inspection which I have recently made of the North Midland Division, under Major-General Hon. Montagu-Stuart-Wortley, and the 2nd London Division, under Major-General Barter.

X. General Baron von Kaulbars, of the Russian General Staff, arrived at my Headquarters on 18 March. He was anxious to study our aviation system, and I gave him every opportunity of doing so. The Bishop of London arrived here with his Chaplain on Saturday, March 27, and left on Monday, April 5.

During the course of his visit to the Army His Lordship was at the front every day, and I think I am right in saying that there was scarcely a unit in the command which was not at one time or another present at his services or addresses.

Personal fatigue and even danger were completely ignored by His Lordship. The Bishop held several services virtually under shell fire, and it was with difficulty that he could be prevented from carrying on his ministrations under rifle fire in the trenches.

I am anxious to place on record my deep sense of the good effect produced throughout the Army by this self-sacrificing devotion on the part of the Bishop of London, to whom I feel personally very deeply indebted.

I have once more to remark upon the devotion to duty, courage, and contempt of danger which has characterised the work of the Chaplains of the Army throughout this campaign.

XI. The increased strength of the Force and the gradual exhaustion of the local resources have necessitated a corresponding increase in our demands on the Line of Communications, since we are now compelled to import many articles which in the early stages could be obtained by local purchase. The Directorates concerned have, however, been carefully watching the situation, and all the Administrative Services on the Line of Communications have continued to work with smoothness and regularity, in spite of the increased pressure thrown upon them. In this connection I wish to bring to notice the good service which has been rendered by the Staff of the Base Ports.

The work of the Railway Transport Department has been excellently carried out, and I take this opportunity of expressing my appreciation of the valuable service rendered by the French railway authorities generally, and especially by Colonel Ragueneau, late Directeur des Chemins de Fer, Lieutenant-Colonel Le Hénaff, Directeur des Chemins de Fer, Lieutenant-Colonel Dumont, Commissaire Militaire, Chemin de Fer du Nord, and Lieutenant-Colonel Frid, Commissaire Régulateur, Armée Anglaise.

The Army Postal Service has continued to work well, and at the present time a letter posted in London is delivered at General Headquarters or at the Headquarters of the Armies and Army Corps on the following evening, and reaches an addressee in the trenches on the second day after posting. The delivery of parcels has also been accelerated, and is carried out with regularity and dispatch. XII. His Majesty the King of the Belgians visited the British lines on 8 February and inspected some of the units in reserve behind the trenches.

During the last two months I have been much indebted to His Majesty and his gallant Army for valuable assistance and co-operation in various ways.

XIII. His Royal Highness the Prince of Wales is the bearer of this despatch.

His Royal Highness continues to make most satisfactory progress. During the Battle of Neuve Chapelle he acted on my General Staff as a Liaison Officer. Reports from the General Officers Commanding Corps and Divisions to which he has been attached agree in commending the thoroughness in which he performs any work entrusted to him.

I have myself been very favourably impressed by the quickness with which His Royal Highness has acquired knowledge of the various branches of the service, and the deep interest he has always displayed in the comfort and welfare of the men.

His visits to the troops, both in the field and in hospitals, have been greatly appreciated by all ranks. His Royal Highness did duty for a time in the trenches with the Battalion to which he belongs.

XIV. In connection with the Battle of Neuve Chapelle I desire to bring to Your Lordship's special notice the valuable services of General Sir Douglas Haig, K.C.B., K.C.I.E., K.C.V.O., A.D.C., Commanding the First Army.

I am also much indebted to the able and devoted assistance I have received from Lieutenant-General Sir William Robertson, K.C.B., K.C.V.O., D.S.O., Chief of the General Staff, in the direction of all the operations recorded in this despatch.

I have many other names to bring to notice for valuable, gallant, and distinguished service during the period under review, and these will form the subject of a separate report at an early date.

I have the honour to be,
Your Lordship's most obedient Servant,
J. D. P. French, Field-Marshal,
Commanding-in-Chief, The British Army in the Field.

Dispatch June 15th

From the Field-Marshal Commanding-in-Chief, The British Army in France. To the Secretary of State for War, War Office, London, S.W.
General Headquarters,

June 15, 1915.

My Lord,

I have the honour to report that since the date of my last despatch (April 5, 1915) the Army in France under my command has been heavily engaged opposite both flanks of the line held by the British Forces.

I. In the North the town and district of Ypres have once more in this campaign been successfully defended against vigorous and sustained attacks made by large forces of the enemy, and supported by a mass of heavy and field artillery, which, not only in number, but also in weight and calibre, is superior to any concentration of guns which has previously assailed that part of the line.

In the South a vigorous offensive has again been taken by troops of the First Army, in the course of which a large area of entrenched and fortified ground has been captured from the enemy, whilst valuable support has been afforded to the attack which our Allies have carried on with such marked success against the enemy's positions to the east of Arras and Lens.

II. I much regret that during the period under report the fighting has been characterised on the enemy's side by a cynical and barbarous disregard of the well-known usages of civilised war and a flagrant defiance of the Hague Convention.

All the scientific resources of Germany have apparently been brought into play to produce a gas of so virulent and poisonous a nature that any human being brought into contact with it is first paralysed and then meets with a lingering and agonising death.

The enemy has invariably preceded, prepared, and supported his attacks by a discharge in stupendous volume of these poisonous gas fumes whenever the wind was favourable.

Such weather conditions have only prevailed to any extent in the neighbourhood of Ypres, and there can be no doubt that the effect of these poisonous fumes materially influenced the operations in that theatre, until experience suggested effective counter measures, which have since been so perfected as to render them innocuous.

The brain power and thought which has evidently been at work before this unworthy method of making war reached the pitch of efficiency which has been demonstrated in its practice shows that the Germans must have harboured these designs for a long time.

As a soldier I cannot help expressing the deepest regret and some surprise that an Army which hitherto has claimed to be the chief exponent of the chivalry of war should have stooped to employ such devices against brave and gallant foes.

III. On the night of Saturday, April 17, a commanding hill which afforded the enemy excellent artillery observation towards the West and North-West was successfully mined and captured.

This hill, known as Hill 60, lies opposite the northern extremity of the line held by the 2nd Corps. The operation was planned and the mining commenced by Major-General Bulfin before the ground was handed over to the troops under Lieutenant-General Sir Charles Fergusson, under whose supervision the operation was carried out.

The mines were successfully fired at 7 p.m. on the 17th, and immediately afterwards the hill was attacked and gained, without difficulty, by the 1st Battalion, Royal West Kent Regiment, and the 2nd Battalion, King's Own Scottish Borderers. The attack was well supported by the Divisional Artillery, assisted by French and Belgian batteries.

During the night several of the enemy's counterattacks were repulsed with heavy loss, and fierce hand-to-hand fighting took place; but on the early morning of the 18th the enemy succeeded in forcing back the troops holding the right of the hill to the reverse slope, where, however, they hung on throughout the day.

On the evening of the 18th these two battalions were relieved by the 2nd Battalion, West Riding Regiment, and the 2nd Battalion, King's Own Yorkshire Light Infantry, who again stormed the hill under cover of heavy artillery fire, and the enemy was driven off at the point of the bayonet. In this operation 53 prisoners were captured, including four officers.

On the 20th and following days many unsuccessful attacks by the enemy were made on Hill 60, which was continuously shelled by heavy artillery.

On May 1 another attempt to recapture Hill 60 was supported by great volumes of asphyxiating gas, which caused nearly all the men along a front of about 400 yards to be immediately struck down by its fumes.

The splendid courage with which the leaders rallied their men and subdued the natural tendency to panic (which is inevitable on such occasions), combined with the prompt intervention of supports, once more drove the enemy back.

A second and more severe "gas" attack, under much more favourable weather conditions, enabled the enemy to recapture this position on May 5.

The enemy owes his success in this last attack entirely to the use of asphyxiating gas. It was only a few days later that the means, which have since proved so effective, of counteracting this method of making war were put into practice. Had it been otherwise, the enemy's attack on May 5 would most certainly have shared the fate of all the many previous attempts he had made.

IV. It was at the commencement of the Second

Battle of Ypres on the evening of April 22, referred to in paragraph I. of this report, that the enemy first made use of asphyxiating gas.

Some days previously I had complied with General Joffre's request to take over the trenches occupied by the French, and on the evening of the 22nd the troops holding the lines east of Ypres were posted as follows:—From Steenstraate to the east of Langemarck, as far as the Poelcappelle Road, a French Division.

Thence, in a south-easterly direction towards the Passchendaele-Becelaere Road, the Canadian Division.

Thence a Division took up the line in a southerly direction east of Zonnebeke to a point west of Becelaere, w hence another Division continued the line southeast to the northern limit of the Corps on its right.

Of the 5th Corps there were four battalions in Divisional Reserve about Ypres; the Canadian Division had one battalion in Divisional Reserve, and the 1st Canadian Brigade in Army Reserve. An Infantry Brigade, which had just been withdrawn after suffering heavy losses on Hill 60, was resting about Vlamertinghe.

Following a heavy bombardment, the enemy attacked the French Division at about 5 p.m., using asphyxiating gases for the first time. Aircraft reported that at about 5 p.m. thick yellow smoke had been seen issuing from the German trenches between Langemarck and Bixschoote. The French reported that two simultaneous attacks had been made east of the Ypres-Staden Railway, in which these asphyxiating gases had been employed.

What follows almost defies description. The effect of these poisonous gases was so virulent as to render the whole of the line held by the French Division mentioned above practically incapable of any action at all. It was at first impossible for anyone to realise what had actually happened. The smoke and fumes hid everything from sight, and hundreds of men were thrown into a comatose or dying condition, and within an hour the whole position had to be abandoned, together with about 50 guns.

I wish particularly to repudiate any idea of attaching the least blame to the French Division for this unfortunate incident.

After all the examples our gallant Allies have shown of dogged and tenacious courage in the many trying situations in which they have been placed throughout the course of this campaign it is quite superfluous for me to dwell on this aspect of the incident, and I would only express my firm conviction that, if any troops in the world had been able to hold their trenches in the face of such a treacherous and altogether unexpected onslaught, the French Division would have stood firm.

The left flank of the Canadian Division was thus left dangerously exposed to serious attack in flank, and there appeared to be a prospect of their being overwhelmed and of a successful attempt by the Germans to cut off the British troops occupying the salient to the East.

In spite of the danger to which they were exposed the Canadians held their ground with a magnificent display of tenacity and courage; and it is not too much to say that the bearing and conduct of these splendid troops averted a disaster which might have been attended with the most serious consequences.

They were supported with great promptitude by the reserves of the Divisions holding the salient and by a Brigade which had been resting in billets.

Throughout the night the enemy's attacks were repulsed, effective counter- attacks were delivered, and at length touch was gained with the French right, and a new line was formed.

The 2nd London Heavy Battery, which had been attached to the Canadian Division, was posted behind the right of the French Division, and, being involved in their retreat, fell into the enemy's hands. It was recaptured by the Canadians in their counter-attack, but the guns could not be withdrawn before the Canadians were again driven back.

During the night I directed the Cavalry Corps and the Northumbrian Division, which was then in general reserve, to move to the west of Ypres, and placed these troops at the disposal of the General Officer Commanding the Second Army. I also directed other reserve troops from the 3rd Corps and the First Army to be held in readiness to meet eventualities.

In the confusion of the gas and smoke the Germans succeeded in capturing the bridge at Steenstraate and some works south of Lizerne, all of which were in occupation by the French. The enemy having thus established himself to the west of the Ypres Canal, I was somewhat apprehensive of his succeeding in driving a wedge between the French and Belgian troops at this point. I directed, therefore, that some of the reinforcements sent north should be used to support and assist General Putz, should he find difficulty in preventing any further advance of the Germans west of the canal.

At about 10 o'clock on the morning of the 23rd connection was finally ensured between the left of the Canadian Division and the French right, about eight hundred yards east of the canal; but as this entailed the maintenance by the British troops of a much longer line than that which they had held before the attack commenced on the previous night, there were no reserves available for counter-attack until reinforcements, which were ordered up from the Second Army, were able to deploy to the east of Ypres.

Early on the morning of the 23rd I went to see General Foch, and from him I received a detailed account of what had happened, as reported by General Putz. General Foch informed me that it was his intention to make good the original line and regain the trenches which the French Division had lost. He expressed the desire that I should maintain my present line, assuring me that the original position would be re-established in a few days. General Foch further informed me that he had ordered up large French reinforcements, which were now on their way, and that troops from the North had already arrived to reinforce General Putz.

I fully concurred in the wisdom of the General's wish to re-establish our old line, and agreed to co-operate in the way he desired, stipulating, however, that if the position was not re-established within a limited time I could not allow the British troops to remain in so exposed a situation as that which the action of the previous twenty-four hours had compelled them to occupy.

During the whole of the 23rd the enemy's artillery was very active, and his attacks all along the front were supported by some heavy guns which had been brought down from the coast in the neighbourhood of Ostend. The loss of the guns on the night of the 22nd prevented this fire from being kept down, and much aggravated the situation. Our positions, however, were well maintained by the vigorous counter-attacks made by the 5th Corps.

During the day I directed two Brigades of the 3rd Corps and the Lahore Division of the Indian Corps to be moved up to the Ypres area and placed at the disposal of the Second Army. In the course of these two or three days many circumstances combined to render the situation east of the Ypres Canal very critical and most difficult to deal with. The confusion caused by the sudden retirement of the French Division, and the necessity for closing up the gap and checking the enemy's advance at all costs, led to a mixing up of units and a sudden shifting of the areas of command which was quite unavoidable. Fresh units, as they came up from the South, had to be pushed into the firing line in an area swept by artillery fire, which, owing to the capture of the French guns, we were unable to keep down.

All this led to very heavy casualties, and I wish to place on record the deep admiration which I feel for the resource and presence of mind evinced by the leaders actually on the spot. The parts taken by Major-General Snow and Brigadier-General Hull were reported to me as being particularly marked in this respect.

An instance of this occurred on the afternoon of the 24th, when the enemy succeeded in breaking through the line at St. Julien. Brigadier-General Hull, acting under the orders of Lieutenant-General Alderson, organised a powerful counter-attack with his own Brigade and some of the nearest available units. He was called upon to control, with only his Brigade Staff, parts of battalions from six separate divisions which were quite new to the ground. Although the attack did not succeed in retaking St. Julien, it effectually checked the enemy's further advance.

It was only on the morning of the 25th that the enemy were able to force back the left of the Canadian Division from the point where it had originally joined the French line. During the night and the early morning of the 25th the enemy directed a heavy attack against the Division at Broodseinde cross-roads, which was supported by a powerful shell fire, but he failed to make any progress. During the whole of this time the town of Ypres and all the roads to the east and west were uninterruptedly subjected to a violent artillery fire, but in spite of this the supply of both food and ammunition was maintained throughout with order and efficiency.

During the afternoon of the 25th many German prisoners were taken, including some officers. The hand-to-hand fighting was very severe, and the enemy suffered heavy loss. During the 26th the Lahore Division and a Cavalry Division were pushed up into the fighting line, the former on the right of the French, the latter in support of the 5th Corps. In the afternoon the Lahore Division, in conjunction with the French right, succeeded in pushing the enemy back some little distance toward the north, but their further advance was stopped owing to the continual employment by the enemy of asphyxiating gas.

On the right of the Lahore Division the Northumberland Infantry Brigade advanced against St. Julien and actually succeeded in entering, and for a time occupying, the southern portion of that village. They were, however, eventually driven back, largely owing to gas, and finally occupied a line a short way to the south. This attack was most successfully and gallantly led by Brigadier- General Riddell, who, I regret to say, was killed during the progress of the operation. Although no attack was made on the south-eastern side of the salient, the troops operating to the east of Ypres were subjected to heavy artillery fire from this direction which took some of the battalions, which were advancing north to the attack, in reverse. Some gallant attempts made by the Lahore Division on the 27th, in conjunction with the French, pushed the enemy further north; but they were partially frustrated by the constant fumes of gas to which they were exposed. In spite of this, however, a certain amount of ground was gained.

The French had succeeded in retaking Lizerne, and had made some progress at Steenstraate and Het Sas; but up to the evening of the 28th no further progress had been made toward the recapture of the original line.

I sent instructions, therefore, to Sir Herbert Plumer,* who was now in charge of the operation, to take preliminary measures for the retirement to the new line which had been fixed upon. On the morning of the 29th I had another interview with General Foch, who informed me that strong reinforcements were hourly arriving to support General Putz, and urged me to postpone issuing orders for any retirement until the result of his attack, which was timed to commence at daybreak on the 30th, should be known. To this I agreed, and instructed Sir Herbert Plumer accordingly.

* Sir Herbert Plumer, who took over the command of Sir Horace Smith-Dorrien, achieved fame by his relief of Mafeking and the operations in the region before the relief.

No substantial advance having been made by the French, I issued orders to Sir Herbert Plumer at one o'clock on May 1 to commence his withdrawal to the new line. The retirement was commenced the following night, and the new line was occupied on the morning of May 4.

I am of opinion that this retirement, carried out deliberately with scarcely any loss, and in the face of an enemy in position, reflects the greatest possible credit on Sir Herbert Plumer and those who so efficiently carried out his orders.

The successful conduct of this operation was the more remarkable from the fact that on the evening of 2 May, when it was only half completed, the enemy made a heavy attack, with the usual gas accompaniment, on St. Julien and the line to the west of it.

An attack on a line to the east of Fortuin was made at the same time under similar conditions. In both cases our troops were at first driven from their trenches by gas fumes, but on the arrival of the supporting battalions and two brigades of a Cavalry Division, which were sent up in support from about Potijze, all the lost trenches were regained at night.

On 3 May, while the retirement was still going on, another violent attack was directed on the northern face of the salient. This was also driven back with heavy loss to the enemy.

Further attempts of the enemy during the night of the 3rd to advance from the woods west of St. Julien were frustrated entirely by the fire of our artillery.

During the whole of the 4th the enemy heavily shelled the trenches we had evacuated, quite unaware that they were no longer occupied. So soon as the retirement was discovered the Germans commenced to entrench opposite our new line and to advance their guns to new positions. Our artillery, assisted by aeroplanes, caused him considerable loss in carrying out these operations.

Up to the morning of the 8th the enemy made attacks at short intervals, covered by gas, on all parts of the line to the east of Ypres, but was everywhere driven back with heavy loss.

Throughout the whole period since the first break of the line on the night of 22 April all the troops in this area had been constantly subjected to violent artillery bombardment from a large mass of guns with an unlimited supply of ammunition. It proved impossible whilst under so vastly superior fire of artillery to dig efficient trenches, or to properly reorganise the line, after the confusion and demoralisation caused by the first great gas surprise and the subsequent almost daily gas attacks. Nor was it until after this date (8 May) that effective preventives had been devised and provided. In these circumstances a violent bombardment of nearly the whole of the 5th Corps front broke out at 7 a.m. on the morning of the 8th, which gradually concentrated on the front of the Division between north and south of Frezenberg. This fire completely obliterated the trenches and caused enormous losses.

The artillery bombardment was shortly followed by a heavy infantry attack, before which our line had to give way.

I relate what happened in Sir Herbert Plumer's own words:—

"The right of one Brigade was broken about 10.15 a.m.; then its centre, and then part of the left of the Brigade in the next section to the south. The Princess Patricia's Canadian Light Infantry, however, although suffering very heavily, stuck to their fire or support trenches throughout the day. At this time two battalions were moved to General Headquarters 2nd line astride the Menin road to support and cover the' left of their Division.

"At 12.25 p.m. centre of a Brigade further to the left also broke; its right battalion, however, the 1st Suffolks, which had been refused to cover a gap, still held on and were apparently surrounded and overwhelmed. Meanwhile, three more battalions had been moved up to reinforce, two other battalions were moved up in support to General Headquarters line, and an Infantry Brigade came up to the grounds of Vlamertinghe Chateau in Corps Reserve.

"At 11.30 a.m. a small party of Germans attempted to advance against the left of the British line, but were destroyed by the 2nd Essex Regiment.

"A counter attack was launched at 3.30 p.m. by the 1st York and Lancaster Regiment, 3rd Middlesex Regiment, 2nd East Surrey Regiment, 2nd Royal Dublin Fusiliers, and the 1st Royal Warwickshire Regiment. The counter attack reached Frezenberg, but was eventually driven back and held up on a line running about north and south through Verlorenhoek, despite repeated efforts to advance. The 12th London Regiment on the left succeeded at great cost in reaching the original trench line, and did considerable execution with their machine gun.

"The 7th Argyll and Sutherland Highlanders and the 1st East Lancashire Regiment attacked in a northeasterly direction towards Wieltje, and connected the old trench line with the ground gained by the counterattack, the line being consolidated during the night.

"During the night orders were received that two Cavalry Divisions would be moved up and placed at the disposal of the 5th Corps, and a Territorial Division would be moved up to be used if required.

"On the 9th the Germans again repeated their bombardment. Very heavy shell fire was concentrated for two hours on the trenches of the 2nd Gloucestershire Regiment and 2nd Cameron Highlanders, followed by an infantry attack which was successfully repulsed. The Germans again bombarded the salient, and a further attack in the afternoon succeeded in occupying 150 yards of trench. The Gloucesters counter-attacked, but suffered heavily, and the attack failed. The salient being very exposed to shell fire from both flanks, as well as in front, it was deemed advisable not to attempt to retake the trench at night, and a retrenchment was therefore dug across it.

"At 3 p.m. the enemy started to shell the whole front of the centre Division, and it was reported that the right Brigade of this Division was being heavily punished, but continued to maintain its line.

"The trenches of the Brigades on the left centre were also heavily shelled during the day, and attacked by infantry. Both attacks were repulsed.

"On the 10th instant the trenches on either side of the Menin-Ypres Road were shelled very severely all the morning. The 2nd Cameron Highlanders, 9th Royal Scots, and the 3rd and 4th King's Royal Rifles, however, repulsed an attack made, under cover of gas, with heavy loss. Finally, when the trenches had been practically destroyed and a large number of the garrison buried, the 3rd King's Royal Rifles and 4th Rifle Brigade fell back to the trenches immediately west of Bellewaarde Wood. So heavy had been the shell fire that the proposal to join up the line with a switch through the wood had to be abandoned, the trees broken by the shells forming an impassable entanglement.

"After a comparatively quiet night and morning (10th-11th) the hostile artillery fire was concentrated on the trenches of the 2nd Cameron Highlanders and 1st Argyll and Sutherland Highlanders at a slightly more northern point than on the previous day The Germans attacked in force and gained a footing in part of the trenches, but were promptly ejected by a supporting company of the 9th Royal Scots. After a second short artillery bombardment the Germans again attacked about 4.15 p.m., but were again repulsed by rifle and machine-gun fire. A third bombardment followed, and this time the Germans succeeded in gaining a trench—or rather what was left of it—a local counter- attack failing. However, during the night the enemy were again driven out. The trench by this time being practically non-existent, the garrison found it untenable under the very heavy shell fire the enemy brought to bear upon it, and the trench was evacuated. Twice more did the German snipers creep back into it, and twice more they were ejected. Finally, a retrenchment was made, cutting off the salient which had been contested throughout the day. It was won owing solely to the superior weight and number of the enemy's guns, but both our infantry and our artillery took a very heavy toll of the enemy, and the ground lost has proved of little use to the enemy.

"On the remainder of the front the day passed comparatively quietly, though most parts of the line underwent intermittent shelling by guns of various calibres.

"With the assistance of the Royal Flying Corps the 31st Heavy Battery scored a direct hit on a German gun, and the North Midland Heavy Battery got on to some German howitzers with great success.

"With the exception of another very heavy burst of shell fire against the right Division early in the morning, the 12th passed uneventfully.

"On the night of the 12th-13th the line was reorganised, the centre Division retiring into Army Reserve to rest, and their places being taken in the trenches by the two Cavalry Divisions; the Artillery and Engineers of the centre Division forming with them what was known as the 'Cavalry Force' under the command of General De Lisle.

"On the 13th, the various reliefs having been completed without incident, the heaviest bombardment yet experienced broke out at 4.30 a.m., and continued with little intermission throughout the day. At about 7.45 a.m. the Cavalry Brigade astride the railway, having suffered very severely, and their trenches having been obliterated, fell back about 800 yards. The North Somerset Yeomanry on the right of the Brigade, although also suffering severely, hung on to their trenches throughout the day, and actually advanced and attacked the enemy with the bayonet. The Brigade on its right also maintained its position, as did also the Cavalry Division, except the left squadron, which, when reduced to sixteen men, fell back. The 2nd Essex Regiment, realising the situation, promptly charged and retook the trench, holding it till relieved by the Cavalry. Meanwhile a counter-attack by two Cavalry Brigades was launched at 2.30 p.m., and succeeded, in spite of very heavy shrapnel and rifle fire, in regaining the original line of trenches, turning out the Germans who had entered it, and in some cases pursuing them for some distance. But a very heavy shell fire was again opened on them, and they were again compelled to retire to an irregular line in rear, principally the craters of shell holes. The enemy in their counter-attack suffered very severe losses.

"The fighting in other parts of the line was little less severe. The 1st East Lancashire Regiment were shelled out of their trenches, but their support company and the 2nd Essex Regiment, again acting on their own initiative, won them back. The enemy penetrated into the farm at the north-east corner of the line, but the 1st Rifle Brigade, after a severe struggle, expelled them. The 1st Hampshire Regiment also repelled an attack, and killed every German who got within fifty yards of their trenches. The 5th London Regiment, despite very heavy casualties, maintained their position unfalteringly. At the southern end of the line the left Brigade was once again heavily shelled, as indeed was the whole front. At the end of a very hard day's fighting our line remained in its former position, with the exception of the short distance lost by one Cavalry Division. Later, the line was pushed forward, and a new line was dug in a less exposed position, slightly in rear of that originally held. The night passed quietly.

"Working parties of from 1,200 to 1,800 men have been found every night by a Territorial Division and other units for work on rear lines of defence, in addition to the work performed by the garrisons in reconstructing the front line trenches which were daily destroyed by shell fire.

"The work performed by the Royal Flying Corps has been invaluable. Apart from the hostile aeroplanes actually destroyed, our airmen have prevented a great deal of aerial reconnaissance by the enemy, and have registered a large number of targets with our artillery.

"There have been many cases of individual gallantry. As instances may be given the following:—
"During one of the heavy attacks made against our infantry gas was seen rolling forward from the enemy's trenches. Private Lynn* of the 2nd Lancashire Fusiliers at once rushed to the machine gun without waiting to adjust his respirator. Single-handed he kept his gun in action the whole time the gas was rolling over, actually hoisting it on the parapet to get a better field of fire. Although nearly suffocated by the gas, he poured a stream of lead into the advancing enemy and checked their attack. He was carried to his dug-out, but, hearing another attack was imminent, he tried to get back to his gun. Twenty-four hours later he died in great agony from the effects of the gas.

* He was awarded the Victoria Cross for the gallant deed which cost him his life.

"A young subaltern in a cavalry regiment went forward alone one afternoon to reconnoitre. He got into a wood, 1,200 yards in front of our lines, which he found occupied by Germans, and came back with the information that the enemy had evacuated a trench and were digging another—information which proved most valuable to the artillery as well as to his own unit.

"A patrol of two officers and a non-commissioned officer of the 1st Cambridgeshires went out one night to reconnoitre a German trench 350 yards away. Creeping along the parapet of the trench, they heard sounds indicating the presence of six or seven of the enemy. Further on they heard deep snores, apparently proceeding from a dug-out immediately beneath them. Although they knew that the garrison of the trench outnumbered them, they decided to procure an identification.

Unfortunately in pulling out a clasp knife with which to cut off the sleeper's identity disco, one of the officer's revolvers went off. A conversation in agitated whispers broke out in the German trench, but the patrol crept safely away, the garrison being too startled to fire.

"Despite the very severe shelling to which the troops had been subjected, which obliterated trenches and caused very many casualties, the spirit of all ranks remains excellent. The enemy's losses, particularly on the 10th and 13th, have unquestionably been serious. On the latter day they evacuated trenches (in face of the cavalry counter-attack) in which were afterwards found quantities of equipment and some of their own wounded. The enemy have been seen stripping our dead, and on three occasions men in khaki have been seen advancing."

The fight went on by the exchange of desultory shell and rifle fire, but without any remarkable incident until the morning of 24 May. During this period, however, the French on our left had attained considerable success. On the 11th instant they captured Steenstraate and the trenches in Het Sas, and on the 16th they drove the enemy headlong over the canal, finding two thousand German dead. On the 17th they made a substantial advance on the east side of the canal, and on the 20th they repelled a German counter-attack, making a further advance in the same direction, and taking one hundred prisoners.

On the early morning of the 24th a violent outburst of gas against nearly the whole front was followed by heavy shell fire, and the most determined attack was delivered against our position east of Ypres.

The hour the attack commenced was 2.45 a.m. A large proportion of the men were asleep, and the attack was too sudden to give them time to put on their respirators.

The 2nd Royal Irish and the 9th Argyll and Sutherland Highlanders, overcome by gas fumes, were driven out of a farm held in front of the left Division, and this the enemy proceeded to hold and fortify.

All attempts to retake this farm during the day failed, and during the night of the 24th-25th the General Officer Commanding the left Division decided to take up a new line which, although slightly in rear of the old one, he considered to be a much better position. This operation was successfully carried out.

Throughout the day the whole line was subjected to one of the most violent artillery attacks which it had ever undergone; and the 5th Corps and the Cavalry Divisions engaged had to fight hard to maintain their positions. On the following day, however, the line was consolidated, joining the right of the French at the same place as before, and passing through Wieltje (which was strongly fortified) in a southerly direction on to Hooge, where the Cavalry have since strongly occupied the chateau, and pushed our line further east.

V. In pursuance of a promise which I made to the French Commander-in-Chief to support an attack which his troops were making on 9 May between the right of my line and Arras, I directed Sir Douglas Haig to carry out on that date an attack on the German trenches in the neighbourhood of

Rougebanc (north-west of Fromelles) by the 4th Corps, and between Neuve Chapelle and Givenchy, by the 1st and Indian Corps.

The bombardment of the enemy's positions commenced at 5 a.m.

Half-an-hour later the 8th Division of the 4th Corps captured the first line of German trenches about Rougebanc, and some detachments seized a few localities beyond this line. It was soon found, however, that the position was much stronger than had been anticipated, and that a more extensive artillery preparation was necessary to crush the resistance offered by his numerous fortified posts. Throughout the 9th and 10th repeated efforts were made to make further progress. Not only was this found to be impossible, but the violence of the enemy's machine-gun fire from his posts on the flanks rendered the captured trenches so difficult to hold that all the units of the 4th Corps had to retire to their original position by the morning of the 10th.

The 1st and Indian Divisions south of Neuve Chapelle met with no greater success, and on the evening of the 10th I sanctioned Sir Douglas Haig's proposal to concentrate all our available resources on the southern point of attack.

The 7th Division was moved round from the 4th Corps area to support this attack, and I directed the General Officer Commanding the First Army to delay it long enough to ensure a powerful and deliberate artillery preparation.

The operations of the 9th and 10th formed part of a general plan of attack which the Allies were conjointly conducting on a line extending from the north of Arras to the south of Armentières; and, although immediate progress was not made during this time by the British forces, their attack assisted in securing the brilliant successes attained by the French forces on their right, not only by holding the enemy in their front, but by drawing off a part of the German reinforcements which were coming up to support their forces east of Arras.

It was decided that the attack should be resumed on the night of the 12th instant, but the weather continued very dull and misty, interfering much with artillery observation. Orders were finally issued, therefore, for the action to commence on the night of the 15th instant.

On May 15 I moved the Canadian Division into the 1st Corps area and placed them at the disposal of Sir Douglas Haig.

The infantry of the Indian Corps and the 2nd Division of the 1st Corps advanced to the attack of the enemy's trenches which extended from Richebourg L'Avoué in a south-westerly direction. Before daybreak the 2nd Division had succeeded in capturing two lines of the enemy's trenches, but the Indian Corps were unable to make any progress owing to the strength of the enemy's defences in the neighbourhood of Richebourg L'Avoué.

At daybreak the 7th Division, on the right of the 2nd, advanced to the attack, and by 7 a.m. had entrenched themselves on a line running nearly north and south, half-way between their original trenches and La Quinque Rue, having cleared and captured several lines of the enemy's trenches, including a number of fortified posts.

As it was found impossible for the Indian Corps to make any progress in face of the enemy's defences Sir Douglas Haig directed the attack to be suspended at this point, and ordered the Indian Corps to form a defensive flank.

The remainder of the day was spent in securing and consolidating positions which had been won, and endeavouring to unite the inner flanks of the 7th and 2nd Divisions, which were separated by trenches and posts strongly held by the enemy.

Various attempts which were made throughout the day to secure this object had not succeeded at nightfall in driving the enemy back.

The German communications leading to the rear of their positions were systematically shelled throughout the night.

About two hundred prisoners were captured on the 16th instant.

Fighting was resumed at daybreak; and by 11 o'clock the 7th Division had made a considerable advance, capturing several more of the enemy's trenches. The task allotted to this Division was to push on in the direction of Rue D'Ouvert, Chateau St. Roch, and Canteleux.

The 2nd Division was directed to push on when the situation permitted towards the Rue de Marais and Violanes.

The Indian Division was ordered to extend its front far enough to enable it to keep touch with the left of the 2nd Division when they advanced.

On this day I gave orders for the 51st (Highland) Division to move into the neighbourhood of Estaires to be ready to support the operations of the First Army.

At about noon the enemy was driven out of the trenches and posts which he occupied between the two Divisions, the inner flanks of which were thus enabled to join hands.

By nightfall the 2nd and 7th Divisions had made good progress, the area of captured ground being considerably extended to the right by the successful operations of the latter.

The state of the weather on the morning of the 18th much hindered an effective artillery bombardment, and further attacks had, consequently, to be postponed.

Infantry attacks were made throughout the line in the course of the afternoon and evening; but, although not very much progress was made, the line was advanced to the La Quinque Rue-Béthune Road before nightfall.

On May 19 the 7th and 2nd Divisions were drawn out of the line to rest. The 7th Division was relieved by the Canadian Division and the 2nd Division by the 51st (Highland) Division.

Sir Douglas Haig placed the Canadian and 51st Divisions, together with the artillery of the 2nd and 7th Divisions, under the command of Lieutenant-General Alderson, whom he directed to conduct the operations which had hitherto been carried on by the General Officer Commanding First Corps; and he directed the 7th Division to remain in Army Reserve.

During the night of the 19th-20th a small post of the enemy in front of La Quinque Rue was captured.

During the night of the 20th-21st the Canadian Division brilliantly carried on the excellent progress made by the 7th Division by seizing several of the enemy's trenches and pushing forward their whole line several hundred yards. A number of prisoners and some machine guns were captured.

On the 22nd instant the 51st (Highland) Division was attached to the Indian Corps, and the General Officer Commanding the Indian Corps took charge of the operations at La Quinque Rue, Lieutenant-General Alderson with the Canadians conducting the operations to the north of that place.

On this day the Canadian Division extended their line slightly to the right and repulsed three very severe hostile counter-attacks.

On May 24-25 the 47th Division (2nd London Territorial) succeeded in taking some more of the enemy's trenches and making good the ground gained to the east and north.

I had now reason to consider that the battle, which was commenced by the First Army on May 9 and renewed on the 16th, having attained for the moment the immediate object I had in view, should not be further actively proceeded with; and I gave orders to Sir Douglas Haig to curtail his artillery attack and to strengthen and consolidate the ground he had won.

In the battle of Festubert above described the enemy was driven from a position which was strongly entrenched and fortified, and ground was won on a front of four miles to an average depth of 600 yards.

The enemy is known to have suffered very heavy losses, and in the course of the battle 785 prisoners and 10 machine guns were captured. A number of machine guns were also destroyed by our fire. During the period under report the Army under my command has taken over trenches occupied by some other French Divisions.

I am much indebted to General D'Urbal, commanding the 10th French Army, for the valuable and efficient support received throughout the battle of Festubert from three groups of French 75 millimetre guns.

In spite of very unfavourable weather conditions, rendering observation most difficult, our own artillery did excellent work throughout the battle.

VI. During the important operations described above, which were carried on by the First and Second Armies, the 3rd Corps was particularly active in making demonstrations with a view to holding the enemy in its front and preventing reinforcements reaching the threatened area.

As an instance of the successful attempts to deceive the enemy in this respect it may be mentioned that on the afternoon of the 24th instant a bombardment of about an hour was carried out by the 6th Division with the object of distracting attention from the Ypres salient.

Considerable damage was done to the enemy's parapets and wire; and that the desired impression was produced on the enemy is evident from the German wireless news on that day, which stated, "West of Lille the English attempts to attack were nipped in the bud."

In previous reports I have drawn attention to the enterprise displayed by the troops of the 3rd Corps in conducting reconnaissances, and to the courage and resource shown by officers' and other patrols in the conduct of these minor operations.

Throughout the period under report this display of activity has been very marked all along the 3rd Corps front, and much valuable information and intelligence have been collected.

VII. I have much pleasure in again expressing my warm appreciation of the admirable manner in which all branches of the Medical Services now in the field, under the direction of Surgeon-General Sir Arthur Sloggett, have met and dealt with the many difficult situations resulting from the operations during the last two months.

The medical units at the front were frequently exposed to the enemy's fire, and many casualties occurred amongst the officers of the regimental Medical Service. At all times the officers, non-commissioned officers and men, and nurses carried out their duties with fearless bravery and great devotion to the welfare of the sick and wounded.

The evacuation of casualties from the front to the Base and to England was expeditiously accomplished by the Administrative Medical Staffs at the front and on the Lines of Communication. All ranks employed in units of evacuation and in Base Hospitals have shown the highest skill and untiring zeal and energy in alleviating the condition of those who passed through their hands. The whole organisation of the Medical Services reflects the highest credit on all concerned.

VIII. I have once more to call your Lordship's attention to the part taken by the Royal Flying Corps in the general progress of the campaign, and I wish particularly to mention the invaluable assistance they rendered in the operations described in this report, under the able direction of Major-General Sir David Henderson.

The Royal Flying Corps is becoming more and more an indispensable factor in combined operations. In cooperation with the artillery, in particular, there has been continuous improvement both in the methods and in the technical material employed. The ingenuity and technical skill displayed by the officers of the Royal Flying Corps, in effecting this improvement, have been most marked.

Since my last despatch there has been a considerable increase both in the number and in the activity of German aeroplanes in our front. During this period there have been more than sixty combats in the air, in which not one British aeroplane has been lost. As these fights take place almost invariably over or behind the German lines, only one hostile aeroplane has been brought down in our territory. Five more, however, have been definitely wrecked behind their own lines, and many have been chased down and forced to land in most unsuitable ground.

In spite of the opposition of hostile aircraft, and the great number of anti- aircraft guns employed by the enemy, air reconnaissance has been carried out with regularity and accuracy.

I desire to bring to your Lordship's notice the assistance given by the French Military Authorities, and in particular by General Hirschauer, Director of the French Aviation Service, and his assistants, Colonel Bottieaux and Colonel Stammler, in the supply of aeronautical material, without which the efficiency of the Royal Flying Corps would have been seriously impaired.

IX. In this despatch I wish again to remark upon the exceptionally good work done throughout this campaign by the Army Service Corps and by the Army Ordnance Department, not only in the field, but also on the Lines of Communication and at the Base ports.

To foresee and meet the requirements in the matter of Ammunition, Stores, Equipment, Supplies, and Transport has entailed on the part of the officers, non-commissioned officers, and men of these

Services a sustained effort which has never been relaxed since the beginning of the war, and which has been rewarded by the most conspicuous success.

The close co-operation of the Railway Transport Department, whose excellent work, in combination with the French Railway Staff, has ensured the regularity of the maintenance services, has greatly contributed to this success.

The degree of efficiency to which these Services have been brought was well demonstrated in the course of the Second Battle of Ypres.

The roads between Poperinghe and Ypres, over which transport, supply, and ammunition columns had to pass, were continually searched by hostile heavy artillery during the day and night; whilst the passage of the canal through the town of Ypres, and along the roads east of that town, could only be effected under most difficult and dangerous conditions as regards hostile shell fire. Yet, throughout the whole five or six weeks during which these conditions prevailed, the work was carried on with perfect order and efficiency.

X. Since the date of my last report some Divisions of the "New" Army have arrived in this country.*

He was awarded the Victoria Cross for the gallant deed which cost him his life.

I made a close inspection of one Division, formed up on parade, and have at various times seen several units belonging to others.

These Divisions have as yet had very little experience in actual fighting; but, judging from all I have seen, I am of opinion that they ought to prove a valuable addition to any fighting force.

As regards the Infantry, their physique is excellent, whilst their bearing and appearance on parade reflects great credit on the officers and staffs responsible for their training. The units appear to be thoroughly well officered and commanded. The equipment is in good order and efficient.
Several units of artillery have been tested in the firing line behind the trenches, and 1 hear very good reports of them. Their shooting has been extremely good, and they are quite fit to take their places in the line.

The Pioneer Battalions have created a very favourable impression, the officers being keen and ingenious and the men of good physique and good diggers. The equipment is suitable. The training in field works has been good, but, generally speaking, they require the assistance of Regular Royal Engineers as regards laying out of important works. Man for man in digging the battalions should do practically the same amount of work as an equivalent number of sappers, and in riveting, entanglement, etc., a great deal more than the ordinary infantry battalions.

XI. During the months of April and May several divisions of the Territorial Force joined the Army under my command.

Experience has shown that these troops have now reached a standard of efficiency which enables them to be usefully employed in complete divisional units.

Several divisions have been so employed; some in the trenches, others in the various offensive and defensive operations reported in this despatch.

In whatever kind of work these units have been engaged, they have all borne an active and distinguished part, and have proved themselves thoroughly reliable and efficient.

The opinion I have expressed in former despatches as to the use and value of the Territorial Force has been fully justified by recent events.

XII. The Prime Minister was kind enough to accept an invitation from me to visit the Army in France, and arrived at my Headquarters on May 30.

Mr. Asquith made an exhaustive tour of the front, the hospitals, and all the administrative arrangements made by Corps Commanders for the health and comfort of men behind the trenches. It was a great encouragement to all ranks to see the Prime Minister amongst them; and the eloquent words which on several occasions he addressed to the troops had a most powerful and beneficial effect.

As I was desirous that the French Commander-in-Chief should see something of the British troops, I asked General Joffre to be kind enough to inspect a division on parade.

The General accepted my invitation, and on May 27 he inspected the 7th Division, under the command of Major-General H. de la P. Gough, C.B., which was resting behind the trenches. General Joffre subsequently expressed to me in a letter the pleasure it gave him to see the British troops, and his appreciation of their appearance on parade. He requested me to make this known to all ranks.

The Moderator of the Church of Scotland, the Right Reverend Dr. Wallace Williamson, Dean of the Order of the Thistle, visited the Army in France between May 7 and 17, and made a tour of the Scottish regiments with excellent results.

XIII. In spite of the constant strain put upon them by the arduous nature of the fighting which they are called upon to carry out daily and almost hourly, the spirit which animates all ranks of the Army in France remains high and confident.

They meet every demand made upon them with the utmost cheerfulness.

This splendid spirit is particularly manifested by the men in hospital, even amongst those who are mortally wounded.

The invariable question which comes from lips hardly able to utter a sound is, "How are things going on at the front?"

XIV. In conclusion, I desire to bring to Your Lordship's special notice the valuable services rendered by General Sir Douglas Haig in his successful handling of the troops of the First Army throughout the Battle of Festubert, and Lieutenant-General Sir Herbert Plumer for his fine defence of Ypres throughout the arduous and difficult operations during the latter part of April and the month of May.

I have the honour to be,
Your Lordship's most obedient Servant,
J.D.P. French,
Field-Marshal, Commanding-in-Chief, The British Army in France.

Edgar Wallace – A Short Biography

Richard Horatio Edgar Wallace was born on the 1st April 1875 at 7 Ashburnham Grove, Greenwich. His mother, Mary Jane "Polly" Richards was born into an Irish Catholic family in Liverpool in 1843 and had worked in theatres, both as an actress in bit-parts and as a stagehand and usherette, until she married a Merchant Navy Captain, Joseph Richards, in 1867. He too had been born into an Irish Catholic family in Liverpool. His father had also been a Captain in the Merchant Navy, and his mother's family had a marine background. Mary was eight months pregnant with Joseph's child when he died at sea, and it was once the child had been born that she first turned to the stage, taking the stage name Polly Richards.

She joined the Marriott family theatre troupe in 1872. It was managed by Mrs. Alice Edgar, Richard Edgar, Grace Edgar, Adeline Edgar and Richard Horatio Edgar, Wallace's father. In late 1874 Mary and Richard Horatio Edgar had a brief sexual encounter at the party following a successful show, and she fell pregnant. Worried about the scandal which would ensue and fearing that she might forever lose her job at the troupe, she fabricated an obligation in Greenwich would detain her there for at least six months. She lived in a room in the boarding house on Ashburnham Grove until her son, Edgar, was born. She had already made preparations through her midwife for a couple to foster the child, and when Edgar was born the midwife presented her with Mrs Freeman. Her husband was a fishmonger at Billingsgate market and she already had ten children. She was happy to foster the child and for Polly to make frequent visits to see him in exchange for a small sum of money which Polly made from her work in the theatre troupe.

Wallace was now known as Richard Horatio Edgar Freeman, taking his father's forenames and his foster family's surname. Broadly speaking his childhood was a happy one. The Freemans looked after him lovingly and he had good friendships with his foster siblings, particularly Clara Freeman, twenty years his senior, who often looked after him as a child. After a few years Polly's finances tightened and she was no longer in a position to afford the fee she had been paying the Freemans. However, they had grown to love the young Wallace and opted to adopt him in order to keep him out of the workhouse. Polly could no longer visit him. George Freeman was keen to ensure that he had equal opportunities and did all he could to secure him an education at St. Alfege with St. Peter's, a Peckham boarding school. Despite his adoptive father's efforts, though, Wallace left the school aged twelve for truancy.

Instead he went to work and by the time he was fourteen or fifteen he had experience selling newspapers at Ludgate Circus, near Fleet Street, as a worker in a rubber factory, as a shoe shop assistant, as a milk delivery boy and as a ship's cook. He stole from the milk company which resulted in his dismissal, and in 1894 was engaged to a local girl from Deptford named Edith Anstree, though he broke this off and instead joined the Infantry. He adopted the name Edgar Wallace which he took from Lew Wallace, the author of *Ben-Hur*, and his medical record records a diminutive 33" chest and a stunted growth. his first posting was with the West Kent Regiment in South Africa in 1896, though he did not enjoy military life, arranging to be transferred to the Royal Army Medical Corps. Though this was a less strenuous job, it was also significantly less pleasant and so he again transferred to the Press Corps, which he found suited him far better.

He was in Cape Town in 1898 where he met Rudyard Kipling and was inspired to begin writing and publishing poetry and songs. His first collection of ballads, *The Mission that Failed!* and was enough of a success that in 1899 he paid his way out of the armed forces in order to turn to writing full time. His first work was as a war correspondent for Reuters who kept him in Africa to cover the Boer War, and then for the Daily Mail in 1900 and various other periodicals after that. It was while he was in South Africa that he met and married Ivy Maude Caldecott, who was 21 when they married in 1901, despite her Wesleyan missionary father's strong opposition to the union, for several reasons, one of which was that Wallace's writing was not turning quite the profit he had expected it would. *War and Other Poems* and *Writ in Barracks,* both published in 1900, had not proved as popular as his first collection. Eleanor Clare Hellier Wallace, their first child, died of meningitis in 1903 and, in rather deep debt, they returned to London. Wallace used his contacts with the Daily Mail to get work with them in London, electing to write detective novels as a means of making quick money.

Wallace met Polly, his birth mother, in 1903. He didn't remember her from his childhood as he had been too young when she became unable to visit, so it was as though they were meeting for the first time. She was sixty years old and terminally ill, living in abject poverty. She had come to Wallace seeking financial support, but he turned her away. She died in the Bradford Infirmary later that year. In 1904 he and Ivy had a son, Bryan. He was still writing and had completed his first thriller, *The Four Just Men*. Since nobody would publish it he resorted to setting up his own publishing company which he called Tallis Press and he published a serialised version of *The Four Just Men* in 1905. He received promotional assistance from the Daily Mail in which he ran a competition for entrants to guess the method of murder in the final chapter, with a prize of £1,000 for a correct guess. Although the paper's proprietor, Lord Alfred Harmsworth, refused Wallace the £1,000 prize money, Wallace persisted and went ahead with the competition, recklessly advertising on billboards and buses all over the country, hoping to expand his advertisements across the Empire. His worried colleagues at the Daily Mail managed to convince him to lower the prize money to £500, split into a first prize of £250, a second prize of £200 and a third of £50, but with the total cost of his advertisements nearing £2,000 he would need to sell £2,500 worth of copies before he could see any profit. He was confident that this could be achieved in just three months.

Though he had remarkable enthusiasm, it became clear that his managerial skills left a lot to be desired. It soon emerged that nowhere in the competition terms and conditions had he included a clause limiting the competition to one single winner; instead, any entrant with a winning answer was entitled to their corresponding prize money. Thus, if ten entrants guessed the first prize answer, the competition was obliged to pay each entrant £250. This error was only noticed after the competition had been closed and the solution had been printed in the final installment of the novel, meaning that not only was there no opportunity to write his way out of enormous financial obligation, but the entrants who had guessed correctly would by now have read the final chapter and know they had done so. £250 was an enormous amount of money to the average Edwardian family and those entitled to it were likely to make a lot of noise if they didn't receive their money. Despite this, Wallace's fist instinct was to attempt to ignore the issue entirely, even as he discovered that he initial calculations had been dramatically over-enthusiastic and it would take nearer to two years of continuous sales to break even at the initial cost of £2,500, let alone the new figure which included every correct guesser. Compounding the problem even further was the awful realisation that as sales continued throughout the initial three month period and Wallace approached the £2,500 break-even figure, new readers were still eligible to enter and guess correctly. Though it is unknown how much he eventually owed his readers, Lord Harmsworth found himself having to loan over £5,000 in order to protect the reputation of the newspaper, since 1906 had come around and there still hadn't been a list printed of all prize-winners. It was less a charitable act than one of a man anxious that the failure would reflect ill on his own paper. Wallace filed for bankruptcy shortly thereafter and as a token gesture to his creditors sold the rights to the novel to Sir George Newnes, a publisher and editor, for £75. In the midst of this chaos though, Wallace managed to write and published *Smithy*, which would become the first of a series of *Smithy* novels.

Following this fiascos Wallace was dismissed from the Daily Mail in 1907 when inaccuracies which were found in his reporting, resulting in libel cases being brought against the paper. That year he became the first reporter to be fired from the Daily Mail and was his awful reputation prevented him from finding work at any other papers. Despite all this, though, he travelled to the Congo Free State later that year and reported on the criminal treatment of the Congolese people by King Leopold II of Belgium and the Belgian rubber companies. Up to fifteen million Congolese were killed in various atrocities, and Wallace was asked to serialise stories based on his experiences for her penny magazine *Weekly Tale-Teller*. He and Ivy had another daughter, named Patricia, in 1908. Though his new work for *Weekly Tale-Teller* was bringing in some money, their financial situation was still dire and Ivy was occasionally forced to sell off her jewellery and possessions in order to pay for food. In 1911 his Congolese stories were published in a collection called *Sanders of the River*, which quickly became a bestseller. He would publish eleven more such collections featuring a total of 102 stories of adventure and tribal life set on the river Congo.

From 1908 he started to enjoy a revival of both his success and his reputation. The majority of his initial writing he sold outright in order to make money as quickly as possible and placate his creditors in the United Kingdom and South Africa, but as his success saw the reestablishment of his reputation he began to find work once again as a journalist, beginning in horse racing for the *Week-End*, the *Evening News* and then as an editor for the *Week-End Racing Supplement*. Following this success he started his own racing papers, *Bibury's* and *R. E. Walton's Weekly*, eventually buying his own racehorses and losing thousands gambling. His success was insufficient to support his newly extravagant lifestyle and his marriage began to fail in the light of his financial irresponsibility. He and Ivy had their last child together, Michael Blair Wallace, in 1916, and she filed for divorce in 1918 moving to Tunbridge Wells with her children.

Wallace began to fall for his secretary Ethel Violet King and they married in 1921, having a child, Penelope Wallace, in 1923, who would herself go on to become a successful crime writer. Wallace now began to take his career as a fiction writer more seriously, signing with Hodder and Stoughton in 1921. He now began to organize his contracts more carefully, arranging for royalties and properly organized promotions, run by people more business-minded than himself. He was marketed as the 'King of Thrillers' and they gave him the trademark image of a trilby, a cigarette holder and a yellow Rolls Royce. He was truly prolific, capable not only of producing a 70,000 word novel in three days but of doing three novels in a row in such a manner. His publishers signed off on almost everything he wrote as soon as he turned it in, estimating that by 1928 one in four books being read at any time was written by Wallace, for alongside his famous thrillers he wrote variously in other genres, including but not limited to science fiction, non-fiction accounts of WWI which amounted to ten volumes and screen plays. Eventually he would reach the remarkable total of 170 novels, 18 stage plays and 957 short stories.

Wallace became chairman of the Press Club which to this day holds an annual Edgar Wallace Award, rewarding 'excellence in writing'. In 1923 he broadcasted a report on the Epsom Derby horse race for the British Broadcasting Company, making him the first ever radio sports correspondent. His ex-wife Ivy had suffered from breast cancer between 1923-1924, and it eventually killed her in 1926 despite a successful operation to remove a tumour the year before. He wrote the essay "The Canker in our Midst" in 1926 which dealt, aggressively and controversially, with the problem of paedophilia in show business, describing how children were unwittingly left open to sexual abuse, and linking paedophilia with homosexuality. Its tone has been described as "intolerant, blustering, kick-the-blighters-down-the-stairs". He was appointed chairman of the British Lion Film Corporation on the back of the success of *The Ringer* and on the agreement that he give British Lion first choice on all his future work. This contract gave him an annual salary and a large amount of stock with the company, along with a stipend on all British Lion production of his work and 10% of their annual profits. This extraordinary contract gave him annual earnings by 1929 of almost £50,000, or almost £2 million in 2014.

He now became an active figure in politics, entering the 1931 general election as a Liberal contestant in Blackpool, rejecting the current government in favour of free trade. He lost the election by over 33,000 votes and went to America in late 1931, once again deeply in debt after buying the *Sunday News* which closed six months later. In America he quickly found work as a script doctor for RKO Pictures, enjoying early success with the 1932 adaptation of *The Hound of the Baskervilles*. This success, along with that of the play *The Green Pack*, established his reputation in America and he was able to see his own work adapted for film, beginning with *The Four Just Men*. His most successful theatrical work, *On The Spot*, which explores the life of Al Capone, has been described as "arguably, in construction, dialogue, action, plot and resolution, still one of the finest and purest of 20th-century melodramas". These successes led to his assignation on RKO's "gorilla picture" which would become famous as King Kong in 1933.

He worked on the first draft though he was beginning to experience severe headaches which brought about a diagnosis of diabetes. Despite taking medication to address his condition, it deteriorated in a matter of days. His wife booked him passage home but soon heard that he had entered a coma and died of his condition and double pneumonia on the 7th of February 1932 in North Maple Drive, Beverly Hills. In his honour the bell at St. Bride's church on Fleet Street tolled for the duration of the morning while the flags flew at half-mast. He was buried near his home in England at Chalklands, Bourne End, in Buckinghamshire. Once again, at the time of his death he was in severe debt, mostly to racing bookkeepers, though these debts were settled within two years thanks to the enormous royalties his estate continued to receive from his contracts. His writing has been translated into 29 languages, and is considered one of the most important bodies of Colonial writing.

Edgar Wallace – A Concise Bibliography

African Novels
Sanders of the River (1911)
The People of the River (1911)
The River of Stars (1913)
Bosambo of the River (1914)
Bones (1915)
The Keepers of the King's Peace (1917)
Lieutenant Bones (1918)
Bones in London (1921)
Sandi the Kingmaker (1922)
Bones of the River (1923)
Sanders (1926)
Again Sanders (1928)

Four Just Men (Series)
The Four Just Men (1905)
The Council of Justice (1908)
The Just Men of Cordova (1917)
The Law of the Four Just Men (US title: Again the Three Just Men) (1921)
The Three Just Men (1926)

Again the Three Just Men (US title: The Law of the Three Just Men) (1929) a.k.a. Again the Three

Mr. J. G. Reeder (Series)
Room 13 (1924)
The Mind of Mr. J. G. Reeder (US title: The Murder Book of Mr. J. G. Reeder) (1925)
Terror Keep (1927)
Red Aces (1929)[27]
The Guv'nor and Other Short Stories (US title: Mr. Reeder Returns) (1932)

Detective Sgt. (Inspector) Elk series
The Nine Bears or The Other Man or The Cheaters (1910)
revised as Silinski - Master Criminal (1930)
The Fellowship of the Frog (1925)
The Joker or The Colossus (1926)
The Twister (1928)
The India-Rubber Men (1929)
White Face (1930)

Educated Evans (Series)
Educated Evans (1924)
More Educated Evans (1926)
Good Evans (1927)

Smithy (Series)
Smithy (1905)
Smithy Abroad (1909)
Smithy and The Hun (1915)
Nobby or Smithy's Friend Nobby (1916)

Crime Novels
Angel Esquire (1908)
The Fourth Plague or Red Hand (1913)
Grey Timothy or Pallard the Punter (1913)
The Man Who Bought London (1915)
The Melody of Death (1915)
A Debt Discharged (1916)
The Tomb of T'Sin (1916)
The Secret House (1917)
The Clue of the Twisted Candle (1918)
Down under Donovan (1918)
The Man Who Knew (1918)
The Strange Lapses of Larry Loman (1918)
The Green Rust (1919)
Kate Plus Ten (1919)
The Daffodil Mystery or The Daffodil Murder (1920)
Jack O'Judgment (1920)
The Angel of Terror or The Destroying Angel (1922)
The Crimson Circle (1922)
Mr. Justice Maxwell or Take-A-Chance Anderson(1922)
The Valley of Ghosts (1922)
Captains of Souls (1923)

The Clue of the New Pin (1923)
The Green Archer (1923)
The Missing Million (1923)
The Dark Eyes of London or The Croakers (1924)
Double Dan or Diana of Kara-Kara (US Title) (1924)
The Face in the Night or The Diamond Men or The Ragged Princess (1924)
The Sinister Man (1924)
The Three Oak Mystery (1924)
The Blue Hand or Beyond Recall (1925)
The Daughters of the Night (1925)
The Gaunt Stranger or Police Work (1925) revised as The Ringer (1926)
A King by Night (1925)
The Strange Countess (1925)
The Avenger or The Hairy Arm (1926)
'The Black Abbot (1926)
The Day of Uniting (1926)
The Door with Seven Locks (1926)
The Man from Morocco or Souls In Shadows or The Black (US Title) (1926)
The Million Dollar Story (1926)
The Northing Tramp or The Tramp (1926)
Penelope of the Polyantha (1926)
The Square Emerald or The Woman (1926)
The Terrible People or The Gallows' Hand (1926)
We Shall See! or The Gaol-Breakers (US Title) (1926)
The Yellow Snake or The Black Tenth (1926)
Big Foot (1927)
The Feathered Serpent or Inspector Wade or Inspector Wade and the Feathered Serpent (1927)
Flat 2 (1927)
The Forger or The Counterfeiter (1927)
Terror Keep (1927)
The Hand of Power or The Proud Sons of Ragusa (1927)
The Man Who Was Nobody (1927)
Number Six (1927)
The Squeaker or The Sign of the Leopard or The Squealer (US Title) (1927)
The Traitor's Gate (1927)
The Double (1928)
The Flying Squad (1928)
The Gunner or Gunman's Bluff (US Title) (1928)
Four Square Jane or The Fourth Square (1929)
The Golden Hades or Stamped In Gold or The Sinister Yellow Sign (1929)
The Green Ribbon (1929)
The Calendar (1930)
The Clue of the Silver Key or The Silver Key (1930)
The Lady of Ascot (1930)
The Devil Man or Sinister Street or Silver Steel
or The Life and Death of Charles Peace (1931)
The Man at the Carlton or The Mystery of Mary Grier (1931)
The Coat of Arms or The Arranways Mystery (1931)
On the Spot: Violence and Murder in Chicago (1931)
When the Gangs Came to London or Scotland Yard's Yankee Dick
or The Gangsters Come To London (1932)

The Frightened Lady or The Case of the Frightened Lady or Criminal At Large (1933)
The Green Pack (1933)
The Man Who Changed His Name (1935)
The Mouthpiece (1935)
Smoky Cell (1935)
The Table (1936)
Sanctuary Island (1936)

Other Novels
Captain Tatham of Tatham Island or Eve's Island or The Island of Galloping Gold (1909)
The Duke in the Suburbs (1909)
Private Selby (1912)
"1925" - The Story of a Fatal Peace (1915)
Those Folk of Bulboro (1918)
The Book of all Power (1921)
Flying Fifty-five (1922)
The Books of Bart (1923)
Barbara on Her Own (1926)

Poetry Collections
The Mission That Failed (1898)
War and Other Poems (1900)
Writ In Barracks (1900)

Non-Fiction
Unofficial Despatches of the Anglo-Boer War (1901)
Famous Scottish Regiments (1914)
Field Marshal Sir John French (1914)
Heroes All: Gallant Deeds of the War (1914)
The Standard History of the War – Volumes 1 – 4 (1914)
Kitchener's Army and the Territorial Forces:
The Full Story of a Great Achievement (1915)
Vol. 2-4. War of the Nations (1915)
Vol. 5-7. War of the Nations (1916)
Vol. 8-9. War of the Nations (1917)
Famous Men and Battles of the British Empire (1917)
Tam of the Scouts (1918)
The Real Shell-Man: The Story of Chetwynd of Chilwell (1919)
People or Edgar Wallace by Himself(1926)
The Trial of Patrick Herbert Mahon (1928)
My Hollywood Diary (1932)

Screenplays
King Kong (1932, first draft of original screenplay, 110 pages) While the script was not used in its
entirety, much of it was retained for the final screenplay.
The Hound of the Baskervilles (1932, British film)
The Squeaker (1930, British film)
Prince Gabby (1929, British film)
Mark of the Frog (1928, American film)
The Valley of Ghosts (192

Short Story Collections
The Admirable Carfew (1914)
The Adventure of Heine (1917)
Tam O' the Scouts (1918)
The Fighting Scouts (1919)
Chick (1923)
The Black Avons (1925)
The Brigand (1927)
The Mixer (1927)
This England (1927)
The Orator (1928)
The Thief in the Night (1928)
Elegant Edward (1928)
The Lone House Mystery and Other Stories (Collins and son, 1929)
The Governor of Chi-Foo (1929)
Again the Ringer The Ringer Returns (US Title) (1929)
The Big Four or Crooks of Society (1929)
The Black or Blackmailers I Have Foiled (1929)
The Cat-Burglar (1929)
Circumstantial Evidence (1929)
Fighting Snub Reilly (1929)
For Information Received (1929)
Forty-Eight Short Stories (1929)
Planetoid 127 and The Sweizer Pump (1929)
The Ghost of Down Hill & The Queen of Sheba's Belt (1929)
The Iron Grip (1929)
The Lady of Little Hell (1929)
The Little Green Man (1929)
The Prison-Breakers (1929)
The Reporter (1929)
Killer Kay (1930)
Mrs William Jones and Bill (1930)
Forty Eight Short-Stories (George Newnes Limited ca. 1930)
The Stretelli Case and Other Mystery Stories (1930)
The Terror (1930)
The Lady Called Nita (1930)
Sergeant Sir Peter or Sergeant Dunn, C.I.D. (1932)
The Scotland Yard Book of Edgar Wallace (1932)
The Steward (1932)
Nig-Nog and other humorous stories (1934)
The Last Adventure (1934)
The Woman From the East (1934) Co-written By Robert George Curtis
The Edgar Wallace Reader of Mystery and Adventure (1943)
The Undisclosed Client (1963)

Other
King Kong, with Draycott M. Dell, (1933), 28 October 1933 Cinema Weekly

Plays
An African Millionaire (1904)
The Forest of Happy Dreams (1910)

Dolly Cutting Herself (1911)
The Manager's Dream (1914)
M'Lady (1921)
Double Dan (1926)
The Mystery of room 45 (1926)
A Perfect Gentleman (1927)
The Terror (1927)
Traitors Gate (1927)
The Lad (1928)
The Man Who Changed His Name (1928)
The Squeaker (1928)[27]
The Calendar (1929)
Persons Unknown (1929)
The Ringer (1929)
The Mouthpiece (1930)
On the Spot (1930)
Smoky Cell (1930)
The Squeaker (1930)
To Oblige A Lady (1930)
The Case of the Frightened Lady (1931)
The Old Man (1931)
The Green Pack (1932)
The Table (1932)

www.ingramcontent.com/pod-product-compliance
Lightning Source LLC
Chambersburg PA
CBHW060138050426
42448CB00010B/2194

www.ingramcontent.com/pod-product-compliance
Lightning Source LLC
Chambersburg PA
CBHW060138050426

42448CB00010B/2194